Journey into Fire

David Spangler

Commentary by Julia Spangler

Also by David Spangler

An Introduction to Incarnational Spirituality

Apprenticed to Spirit

Call of the World

Subtle Worlds: *An Explorer's Field Notes*

Facing the Future

Blessing: *The Art and the Practice*

The Call

Parent as Mystic—Mystic as Parent

Everyday Miracles

The Laws of Manifestation

Reflections on the Christ

The Story Tree

Starheart and other Stories

The Flame of Incarnation

World Work

Crafting Home: *Generating the Sacred*

Crafting Relationships: *The Holding of Others*

Partnering with Earth

Midsummer's Journey with the Sidhe

The Soul's Oracle (Card Deck and Manual)

Manifestation: *Creating the life you love*
                    (Card Deck and Manual)

Card Deck of the Sidhe (with Manual)

Conversations with the Sidhe

Rhythms & Hues: *Poems of the Beloved*

DEDICATION

This book is dedicated to the eternal and loving Flame within us and to all who seek to kindle its Fire within themselves and share its Light with the world.

JOURNEY INTO FIRE

Edited by Aidan Spangler
Book Design by Jeremy Berg
Cover Image istockphoto.com

Published by Lorian Press
686 Island View Drive
Camano Island, WA 98282

ISBN: 978-0-936878-76-8

Spangler/David
Journey Into Fire/David Spangler

First Edition April 2015

Printed in the United States of America

0 9 8 7 6 5 4 3 2 1

www.lorian.org

ACKNOWLEDGEMENTS

I would gratefully like to thank all the people who helped me explore and refine these concepts through many classes. I particularly want to thank my beloved wife and partner, Julia, who took on the task of grounding some of the more abstract concepts in practical ways through her commentary in this book. And special thanks to my son, Aidan, who was my editor. As a writer who has had many editors in his career, Aidan is truly one of the best.

Finally I want to thank those of you who will use this book to help introduce people to the essence and gifts of Incarnational Spirituality.

TABLE OF CONTENTS

PROLOGUE:
A VISION

1962 was a momentous year. In business, the first Wall-Mart store was opened. In popular culture, the first James Bond movie, Dr. No, was released and became a huge hit. The Beatles' first song, "Love Me Do," was released, and on television, Johnny Carson took over *The Tonight Show*. It was also the year Marilyn Monroe died.

In civil rights, federal troops and U. S marshals were called in to quell rioting when James Meredith became the first African-American to enroll at the previously segregated University of Mississippi. It was the year the U.S. Navy SEALS were created and the year President Kennedy announced we would put a man on the moon by the end of the decade. Most memorably though, in October of 1962, the world was brought to the brink of thermonuclear war as Kennedy faced down the Russian Premier, Nikita Khrushchev, in the Cuban Missile Crisis.

For me, it was the year I discovered that my life's work wasn't going to be doing research in molecular biology, though I didn't realize it at the time.

I was seventeen and newly graduated from high school. I was living in Phoenix, Arizona, and one day that summer before I went to Arizona State University, I was walking from our apartment to a nearby shopping mall, a distance of a couple of miles. On the way, I passed the home of one of our family friends, an older woman who lived by herself. Seeing me, she invited me in for a cup of iced tea. As it was a hot day, I was glad for the refreshment and happily said yes.

As adults will do when talking with a youth who's just off to college, as we drank our tea she asked me what I was going to study and what my plans for the future were. I was very clear about what I wanted to do: I planned to be a molecular biologist. I had a passion for science and in particular a keen interest in genetic research. I wanted to know what made us tick at a foundational biological level.

I was about to tell her this when suddenly my consciousness

shifted and I found myself in contact with a non-physical being. This in itself was not surprising to me; I'd been aware of and had had contact with the non-physical or subtle dimensions of the earth for as long as I could remember. What did surprise me was the suddenness and the nature of the vision that appeared in front of me before I had a chance to speak.

I saw floating in the air a genderless, generic human figure, looking much like a department store manikin except that it was glowing with a white Light that radiated from within it. At the same time, a voice behind me said, "A new spirituality is emerging, a spirituality of the incarnate person as a being of Light, a radiant source of sacredness and blessing. Your work is to help this spirituality emerge."

My friend knew of my clairvoyant experiences, so when my eyes began focusing on something she couldn't see, she realized I was experiencing something. The vision didn't last long, and when it was over, she asked me what had happened. When I told her, she said, "Well, I guess that answers my question about what you're going to be doing!"

Although it might have answered it for her, it didn't mean that much to me at the time. I didn't reject it but I didn't respond to it either. I was determined to become a molecular biologist. Time enough to think about spiritual things when I was older! But three years later at the age of twenty, I found myself responding to an inner call that led me out of school and into the spiritual work I've been doing for the past fifty years. It also led me into contact with the non-physical being I called "John" who became my mentor, friend and colleague. (I tell the story of my relationship with John, how it came about and the training he offered me in my book *Apprenticed to Spirit*, should you wish a more fulsome version than I'm offering here.)

John and I worked together for nearly thirty years. The concept of an incarnational spirituality never came up as such, but many of its key insights emerged from our association together. For instance, it was he who introduced me to the idea—and the experience—of Self-Light as well as of Sovereignty, two concepts that play an important part in the journey we're about to take. The nature of love was also a much-discussed topic between us; it was John who first told me that the concept of "unconditional love" could be misunderstood and misapplied in a world of boundaries and conditions.

Even though Incarnational Spirituality was never a phrase which he used, the idea of incarnation itself was important to him. He saw the incarnate state as a valued one, and he always championed the importance of the personal consciousness as well as of the transpersonal consciousness. He did not at all subscribe to the idea that we were divided between a "higher" and a "lower" self. He saw each individual as a whole and as a generative source. Indeed, over and over again in the years we worked together, he would insist on viewing the embodied, incarnate life as being as much a source of spiritual energy and blessing as any "higher" state of being. In a metaphor I was to develop many years later, he saw each person as a "star," a source of radiance.

Around 1990, John left because he needed to move on and take up other assignments. The last thing he said to me was "the time is coming for you to begin the work on a spirituality of boundaries and of incarnation." As it happened, nearly another decade passed before I was able to follow up on this suggestion, but when I did, I realized that in the work we had done together, a foundation had been laid that I was then able to build on. It is this foundation that I seek to share with you in this book.

My friend and Lorian colleague, Jeremy Berg, sometimes refers metaphorically to Incarnational Spirituality as a solar system, with the planets being all the various topics and themes it covers or touches upon. If so, the idea of the individual as a sacred, generative source is the sun of this system, the central idea that gives meaning and energy to all the other ideas that flow out from it. This book is a journey into the fire of that "sun".

It is a book of who we are from the perspective of an incarnational spirituality. It is a distillation of many years of teaching this perspective and the skills it offers. Accordingly, it benefits from the experiences, comments, and insights of the hundreds of people who have honored me by taking my classes and going on this journey with me. It is further graced by the participation of my wife, Julia, who has made this journey a joy through her partnership over the years. A woman of deep insight and wisdom, I asked her to write commentaries to each of the chapters to add another voice to my own to help bring these concepts to life.

Although I have benefitted greatly from my partnership with John and with other non-physical beings, all of whom have contributed over the years to my understanding of the spiritual nature of physical life, the true motivation for my work has been the vision I had when I was seventeen. I did not appreciate it at the time, but over the years of working with John and with the subtle worlds, I've come to recognize its importance. John used to say that we as human beings needed to realize "who and what we are." This vision was a symbol of that realization.

There is a sacred fire in us as incarnate beings that radiates a Light into the world. No matter the course or quality of our life, this fire is in each of us. It may be a dim, smoldering ember in some and a bright, radiant flame in others, but it is there in us all for it is lit by the act of incarnation itself. It is at the heart of a spirituality of incarnation, one that does not separate us from spirit or from the Generative Mystery at the heart of the Sacred. Rather it says that we are part of that Mystery, an expression of its generative nature, a source of the sacred fire of life. We each of us have it in us to find this fire and cultivate it, and when we do, we nourish that which makes us most human. It becomes a journey into the wonder, the presence, the creative power of who we are.

I offer you this book as a step on this journey into fire.

A WORD ABOUT THE EXERCISES IN THIS BOOK

At the end of all the chapters except the last one, you will find one or more exercises. These are designed to give you a felt sense of the central topic covered in the preceding chapter. There is nothing magical about them; they are not carved in stone. Since all the chapters refer to qualities that are innate in you, I think of these exercises simply as lenses to allow you to better see what is already there. If a particular exercise doesn't work for you—if, metaphorically, the lens is out of focus for you—then feel free to change or adapt it as long as such changes are in keeping with the objective. In other words, if you wanted to magnify and see a skin cell on your hand but the microscope you're using is out of focus, you don't want to trade it in for a telescope in order to look at the planet Venus. Just find a microscope that works for you but keep the objective in mind.

FELT SENSE

In the various exercises and practices of Incarnational Spirituality, you'll find that in the instructions, you are often asked to discern the felt sense of particular attunement or state of consciousness that is the object of the exercise or practice. This felt sense is a specific configuration of physical sensation, as well as mental and emotional states (such as moods or feelings).

Suppose you're angry at someone and I say to you, "What does this anger feel like in your body?" Turning your attention to your body, you might feel a pressure in your gut or tightness in your back. Your face may feel flushed. You may feel your hands clenching and unclenching. All of these things contribute to the felt sense of the anger.

Or imagine seeing a glorious sunset with the sky filled with rich colors. How does that feel in your body? Your mind? Your emotions? When I see something like that and feel the awe and wonder of it, I can feel as if my body is opening out and becoming larger. I feel more spacious. That is part of the felt sense of the sunset.

Felt sense is like a body language telling you what is going on at an unconscious, preverbal level. By paying attention to the body sensations—to the felt sense—you may find your body giving you information about yourself and your experiences that is healing or at least helpful.

A felt sense can be subtle and not quickly or easily discerned. It may take time just sitting with the body and listening to it, paying attention to it, as you think about or contemplate something about which you'd like the body's response. Felt sense is information, the body talking to you. As I use the term, it's also the unconscious yet deeply aware parts of your mind and heart talking to you as well. And it's a communication that you feel in yourself, which is why it's a *felt* sense.

Once you have this felt sense committed to memory—the "thought-memory" of your mind, the "feeling-memory" of your emotions, and the "muscle-memory" or "physiological-memory" of your body—you can dispense with the exercise itself. In effect, once you have seen and experienced that inner quality or presence for which the exercise is a lens, so that you can recall it when needed, you don't need the exercise itself.

FOCUSING

Back in the Eighties, a psychotherapist, Eugene Gendlin, wrote an excellent little book called *Focusing* in which he introduced the idea of the felt sense and how to work with it. He defined it a little differently than I do, seeing it mainly as a physical counterpart to unconscious emotional states, but his definition is close enough to mine that I began recommending Gendlin's book to my classes. Then one of his students, Ann Weiser Cornell, wrote an equally good and in some ways more accessible book on this topic called *The Power of Focusing*. Now I recommend it as well as or even instead of Gendlin's earlier version. Here are the references:

- *Focusing*, Eugene Gendlin, Bantam Books, 1981
- *The Power of Focusing*, Ann Weiser Cornell, New Harbinger Publications, 1996.

CHAPTER ONE:
SUNS AND GALAXIES

This book is about the sacredness of being human and in particular the sacredness of being embodied as a physical person upon the earth. It's about the sacredness of incarnation.

I'll be using the metaphor of fire to represent this sacredness and its nurturing presence and radiance. What I hope to show you is that this sacred fire is not a thing but a process, an activity, just as physical fire is a process of combustion that releases energy. You and I embody and express this process in a variety of ways. Understanding why and how we do so is part of our journey into this fire.

The challenge is this: can we imagine being sacred? What does it mean to be sacred?

To find out, let's start this journey with one of the largest, more visible "fires" we know: the sun, the star whose energy powers the cycle of life upon the Earth.

The Sun/Satellite System

A common view of the Sacred us that it is at the center of all things, like the central sun of the universe from which all things derive their existence. I characterize this view as a "Sun/Satellite" model. It consists of a single source around which everything else revolves, reflecting its being, much as the planets revolve around the sun and reflect its light. In this worldview, that which is at the center creates the field that holds everything else within itself.

This model is obviously based on observations of the star we call our sun, and it has permeated our thinking and our history. Civilization itself embodies it, with a center (usually a city) and a periphery (the countryside). Human government has reflected this model more often than not as well, with a king, queen, emperor, Pharaoh, dictator, or ruler at the center and everyone else organized around him or her.

This model is deeply engrained in human imagination. In it, the center is privileged and takes precedence over the periphery. It is the source of power, of being, of richness, of rulership and wisdom.

Even in biology, for a long time the nucleus at the center of the cell was considered its most important part, until experiments proved that the cell could get along quite fine without it. In fact, for the cell, most of its vital metabolic functions occur in the cell membrane at the edge of its body.

The sun, while certainly at the center of our solar system, is itself a star, one of billions and billions of other stars that make up the countless galaxies that populate the universe. Like every star, its mass is great enough that it allows for thermonuclear fusion to take place, transforming hydrogen atoms into helium and giving off energy in the process. It has special significance for us because it is the primary source of energy on the physical level that allows life as we know it to exist

Some years ago, I was participating in a workshop in northern California. It was in a lovely wooded area, and during one of the lunch breaks, I took a walk along one of the paths through the surrounding forest. I was walking along, sauntering really, not thinking of anything, just enjoying the beauty around me when suddenly, about a dozen feet in front of me, a shining globe rose out of the earth and hovered in the air before me at a height of about ten feet. It looked like a miniature version of the sun, except that it was green and giving off a wonderful verdant radiance. I could feel a vital energy emanating from it. Just being in its presence made me feel good.

As I stood there, wholly surprised and delighted by this apparition, a voice said, "The earth is also a star. It is a green star of life." As soon as this was said, the sphere disappeared back down into the earth.

Ever since then, I've imagined this green star glowing in the depths of the earth, an "earth-star" radiant with life. Because of this experience, I no longer think of earth simply as a planet, a body that must receive all its energy from an outside source. Instead, it's a source in its own right, a star not of thermonuclear energy but of the energy of consciousness and vitality generated by the interactions of its biosphere.

This gives a different vision of the solar system, one of

partnership and collaboration in which the sun provides a certain kind of energy and the earth provides another. It may be that on subtle levels, all the planets are radiating certain qualities and vibrations not apparent in the physical universe; every planet may be a generative body—a "star"—of some nature. Certainly this is how the planets are seen in astrology.

The larger point is that everything is generative in some manner. We live in a universe of generative beings, just as our sun exists in a cosmos of generative stars. Some stars are larger, some are smaller, some are brighter, some are dimmer, but all stars are radiating as a result of internal processes.

In this context, we are each a star.

I believe that humanity is struggling to shift away from the sun/satellite model of creation and into one that I call a "galactic" model: that of a community of generative, radiant stars with no one star at the center providing energy for all the others. Rather, all stars interact with and energize each other, each contributing its unique presence and energy to the galactic whole. It is a shift from a centralizing perspective, in which one being or organization holds all the significant power and obedience to the center is held as a primary virtue, to a partnership cosmology in which collaboration and co-creation among participants, each of whom has something unique and important to offer, is paramount. Here's a picture illustrating this shift.

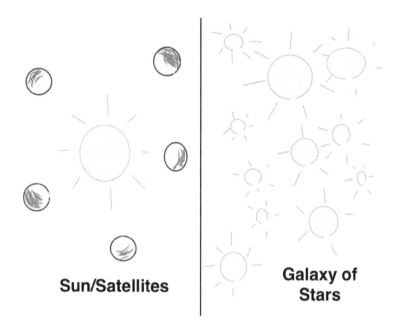

Sun/Satellites

Galaxy of Stars

The sun/satellite perspective privileges the center, which in a theological context means privileging the One as the underlying reality. But a "galactic" perspective honors not just one star but all stars, or perhaps I should say all manifestations of "star-ness" or "starhood." One star may be larger and brighter than another, but this does not privilege it over the other. It is not a "more real" star or a "better" star.

Now I want to be clear that I'm not advancing an argument for polytheism. What I'm actually suggesting is that the Sacred cannot be adequately described as either a single source—a Oneness—nor as multiple sources interacting together. It's something else that embraces and holds both of these manifestations. But how can something be one and many at the same time?

Continuing the metaphor of stars and suns, what makes a star a star is actually the thermonuclear activity which is an expression of the laws of chemistry and physics. These laws, however—especially when taken to a quantum level—don't describe *things*; they describe *relationships*. They describe quantum-level *processes*, all of which can be described mathematically but which are often beyond what we can easily imagine as they have no counterparts in our daily life.

Are these processes only found in one source or are they found in many sources? The answer is both. Our sun as a single star embodies thermonuclear processes that themselves are manifestations of deeper quantum processes. And because it does, our earth receives light and warmth. But our sun is one of uncounted other stars that exhibit the same processes. Physics is at work everywhere.

But quantum processes don't just produce thermonuclear reactions. They also produce all the biological interactions that make organic life possible. They produce the interlocking chains of physical, chemical, and biological interactions that make a biosphere and its ecology possible. Quantum processes in one manifestation produce a sun, in another they produce you and me.

So are there "sacred processes" that in one manifestation produce a unity of being and in another produce individual expressions of sacred beingness that interact to produce a community of sacredness?

I believe there are. Exploring and understanding these processes is largely what Incarnational Spirituality is about.

The exploration is complicated because of our cultural and historical insistence on the primacy of the One. This insistence influences our thoughts about spirituality and how we practice it.

Separation is often thought of as something wrong and out of kilter with the unity of being or the divine oneness. In fact, some spiritual and esoteric traditions speak plainly of the "sin of separation" or the "illusion of separation", for which the cure is an understanding and experience of oneness.

Now, it's clear that there is a truth here. We only have to watch the evening news to see all the ways in which our sense of being separate from each other creates conflict and suffering. The world would be a better place if we had a deeper appreciation of the kinship of all life.

But the challenge here isn't due to separation *per se* but to making separation the primary lens through which the world is viewed; it is a problem arising from *privileging* separation above a sense of oneness as the proper description of the nature of the world.

Suppose instead that separation was one of the "sacred processes". How easy would it be to recognize this if our worldview didn't tell us that the sacred was the oneness and that separation was an illusion or flaw keeping us from that oneness, not to mention a source of suffering in the world? What if we understood that both oneness and separation were complementary processes that enabled the world to come into being, just as nuclear processes enable stars to shine?

Let's consider the idea of duality. Duality is the distinction between the One and the manifold diversity of the universe. More specifically, it's the idea that we are separate from the world, that there is the I and then there is the Other and they are two separate entities. The experience of oneness—so lauded and sought after in many mystical traditions—is contrasted with the everyday sense of multiplicity and otherness. The teaching of duality usually presumes that the One is the reality and the sense of I/Other or the experience of multiplicity is an illusion, in which case the "road to enlightenment" and the path of spiritual practice is to dispel that illusion and blend with the One.

But what if the duality is not the experience of "I and Other" that can be "cured" by Oneness but rather that creation (or the Generative Mystery that is the Sacred) is both One and Many, just as in quantum mechanics light in the form of a photon can be both a particle and a wave? Then the "cure" isn't to dissolve one into the other but to hold both in a co-creative tension, that is to say, in a relationship. This relationship may in fact be one of the "sacred processes", but we can't explore it properly if we believe we have to get rid of it by collapsing one side into the other or we believe that one side is real and the other isn't. A co-creative, generative relationship is not served by privileging one side over the other.

By the way, the well-known phenomenon of light being both particle and wave is often misunderstood. The "reality" isn't that light is both a particle and a wave, that is, that it is simultaneously two contradictory manifestations, but that it is neither. Whatever light "really" is, it's beyond this duality; it's not a particle or a wave but something that is neither but which is capable of being either depending on what is needed. In other words, we have a relationship again, this time between light (whatever it is) and its environment or circumstances. In certain environments and circumstances, it needs to act like a particle, so it does, whereas in other environments and circumstances, it needs to act like a wave, so it does. It has a capacity to relate to what is needed and form the appropriate relationship or manifestation.

Perhaps this capacity is one of the sacred processes, one that we might miss if we insist that the Sacred must be one thing or another. Whatever the Sacred is, it may be neither the One nor the Many, neither a Oneness nor a Diversity, but rather the capacity to be either as needed.

The shift in thinking here is really one of viewing the sacred not simply as a thing or a condition but also as an activity. We are sacred when we are performing this activity.

I don't have to understand what light is in order to use it. I don't have to be a quantum physicist to operate a flashlight. I just need to know how to turn it on. Similarly, I don't have to understand the Sacred in order to express sacredness. I just need to know what activity "turns it on" and to realize that this activity is as much a part of my physical, incarnate state as it is part of a higher dimension of non-physical spirit.

The key point is that sacredness is a function or activity distributed throughout creation, much as thermonuclear activity is distributed throughout the universe of stars. The cosmos may be a oneness but it is also a multitude, and each individual entity within the "Many", be it a person, a planet, a star, an atom, or anything else, participates in the activity of being sacred and in this way becomes a generative source of sacredness within creation.

EXERCISES FOR CHAPTER ONE

Being a Sun

These two exercises are about exploring imaginatively the difference in the felt sense between a sun/satellite relationship and a "galactic" or collaborative one. Each begins in the same way with you sitting in a familiar room in your home, a room which you have furnished and which contains objects of your choosing. The object of the exercise is to experience the same room in two different ways, paying attention to the felt sense of each style of perception.

The first exercise is about being a sun—a radiant center—to your room and the things in it.

- Pick a room in your home and sit in it so that you can see most of the room and the things in it.
- Take a moment to appreciate that this room looks the way it does because of you and choices you have made. The room has a character that exists because of you. It reflects who you are in some manner.
- Pick four objects in the room that are present because of your choices and actions. These are objects that you have selected to be in the room and which contribute to the character of the room overall. They are objects whose meaning and purpose in the room, whether functional or purely decorative, derives from your intent and creativity.
- Pay attention to each of these objects in turn, seeing it as a reflection of your purposes, an embodiment of your intent. Its existence in the room is entirely the result of who you are and your choices. What does this feel like?
- What is the felt sense of your relationship to each of these objects? What is the felt sense of your relationship to the room as a whole?
- Like the sun in the solar system, imagine yourself radiating love to each of these objects and to the room around you as a whole. This love is a blessing of energy and presence rippling out in a circle of Light from you at the center.

- Pay attention to any sensations you have while doing this. Do you feel any response from the objects around you? What do you imagine they may be feeling energetically as they are bathed in your light, your love, and your blessing? What felt sense do you experience as you do this?
- When you feel complete, give thanks to the objects who shared this exercise with you and to the room as a whole and everything within it. Get up and record any impressions, images, sensations, and so forth that may have come to you while doing this exercise.

Being a Galaxy

Don't do this exercise right away immediately after doing the first one. Give yourself and the room a chance to "cool down", so to speak. But after some time has passed (and it doesn't have to be long time--maybe enough for you to get a cup of tea or coffee!), go back to room and sit down as before.

- Take a moment to see the room as it is, independent of you. The room has its own unique character. Take a moment to appreciate it.
- Identify the objects you used in the first part of the exercise. Locate each one in turn and look at it. Appreciate it for what it is in its own being, its own isness.
- Appreciate that each of these objects is itself a manifestation of sacredness. Become aware of the flame of that sacredness within each one. Imagine that it begins to glow with its own internal fire of presence and love.
- Be aware that not only the four objects you have selected are glowing with their own innate sacredness, but the room itself is filled with a glow emanating from all the objects within it.
- Feel your chosen objects—and the room itself as a whole—radiating love and light to you. They are like miniature suns, and you are receiving the radiation of their sacred presence. In turn, your own sacredness responds, so that you, too, are a

radiant source along with them. Take a moment to appreciate this. What does it feel like to you? What is the felt sense of this participation in a community of radiance?

- Just experience the Light in the room that does not come from any particular single source but is the collaborative result of the radiance of everything in the room. What is the felt sense of this? How does it feel different from what you experienced in Part 1 of this exercise?

- Now move around the room, stopping for a moment in different spots. As you do so, feel how the pattern you form with the four objects you have selected (as well as with everything else in the room) changes. As you move, you form different "constellations" with these objects. You may come closer to some objects than you were and further away from others. Does this change anything? If so, how?

- As you move about the room, feel how the patterns shift as you do so, and yet the radiance is the same, adjusting itself as you move so that wherever you are, you receive the blessing from each of the objects, and they receive blessing from you as a fellow "star." What does this feel like?

- When you feel complete, give thanks to the objects who shared this exercise with you and to the room as a whole and everything within it. Get up and record any impressions, images, sensations, and so forth that may have come to you while doing this exercise.

What differences, if any, did you experience between these two exercises, that is, between being the central "sun" of your room and being one of many "stars" in the room?

Julia's Commentary

The heart of this discussion is the recognition first that the Sacred is the source of all of creation and second, as source, it permeates all things, including ourselves. We commonly talk of oneness as a desirable state of consciousness: being one with all life or one with God. I have met many people who have experienced Oneness, but it is fleeting and they feel loss, separation and longing to find it again when the experience ends. I have often heard people express unhappiness at being in embodiment, and longing to go "home", back to that oneness of spirit which seems to have ended with birth. If I see myself as separate, with a sense of being incomplete or of having fallen out of grace, and am filled with longing to return home to the Oneness, then much of my life will be directed to satisfying that longing. This can take the form of a spiritual quest, or as often happens, of pursuit of experiences, substances or relationships that will fill the void I am feeling. If I see myself in a state of separateness, I may define myself as being on a journey of return to my true home, or as lost and trying to find my way, trying to escape the limitations of embodiment.

But when I think of myself as being a sacred source and that the Mystery is an inherent part of my life and soul—born with me at my birth from the foundations of my soul and also meeting me in the life of the cells of my body—then I feel not a longing for lost radiance but radiant from within. As David has described, it is a shift of perspective and self definition which leads to other positive and creative changes in one's life. If I think I am separate, then I will focus on that experience, and I will see the evidence of my separateness in the world around me. How I think will color my perceptions. But if I know that I am part of the Source, that the wave that is the Sacred Mystery is also the particle that is me, I can experience my life as a blessing to the life in the world around me. I know myself as a generative source, akin to a sun or star, and I know all of life is sacred.

To quote David, the One is also the many. If all that is around me, people, trees, mountains, things in my house, are partners in

11

radiance, blessing and being blessed, then where is there separation? This world is also an embodiment of the Divine which is "as close as hands and feet". If I see myself as a sacred particle - a star - and a generative source of sacredness, then I don't have to go anywhere. Where I am, home is, for I carry within me the qualities of "Home". Liberated from any sense of separation, I can get on with creating home here and being a source of home, of love and grace, for the life around me. Such a simple and practical change of perspective can change my life and positively affect the lives of those around me.

In doing the exercise, the feeling of beaming a radiance of love to something is a practice which can be carried into all parts of my day. I can love the life in the dishes I do, in the house that I clean, in the computer I type on, in the people I engage with. If I do this, then sacredness will radiate back to me from the things around me and I can open my senses to the return of that blessing. As I love, so also does the love return. With an inanimate thing, it is as though the love I give, the radiance I send to it, stirs the life source within it, reminding it of its own radiance, and it then bathes me. We enhance each other. With people, my recognition of the radiant source in the stranger in the store seems to light them up, and they radiate back. How can I not feel at home in such a sharing of presence?

CHAPTER TWO:
THE PAPER TOWEL UNIVERSE

The One and the Many represent two different sides of the Mystery of the Sacred. In this case, the "Many" can also be described as a diversity of different individuals or particles. In effect, what we have is the One and the Ones, a multiplicity of "ones". But why? What is the value of the individual? Why does the cosmos have this granular aspect to it?

Once many years ago, one of my non-physical colleagues said to me:

> *The creative process begins with a boundary that allows difference to exist. This difference — that is, the existence of difference — becomes the "engine" of further creation and unfoldment. Where differences meet, something new and potentially unexpected can arise. New information is produced, and new learning can take place. New possibilities appear. To us, this phenomenon of emergence is at the heart of the Sacred. The Sacred does not create as much as it unfolds. It discovers and knows itself through emergence.*

In other words, when you and I relate, because we are different and do not see the world in exactly the same way, we can each learn things we didn't know before by seeing the world through each other's eyes. You have experiences and information that I do not, and vice versa. When we put our heads together, insights may emerge that neither of us could have produced on our own, insights that may surprise us but which will certainly broaden our individual perspectives. The universe in which we live becomes a larger place for each of us than it was before we interacted.

This perspective of the importance of differences led me to postulate what I call the "paper towel" theory of consciousness and sacredness.

Spill some water on a table and blot it up with an ordinary sheet of printer paper. It will absorb some of the water, but much will remain behind. Now spill an equal amount of water on the table and blot it up with a paper towel of the same size as the printer paper. Much more, if not all, of the water will be absorbed. Why?

The pieces of paper are the same size, but a paper towel is ridged or has very tiny bumps all over it. This gives it much more surface area with which to absorb things than the ordinary printer paper has.

Differentiation into the "Many" — i.e. into a multiplicity of "ones" — gives the Sacred more "surface area" with which to interact with creation — or with creative possibilities. Here's a picture of what I mean:

PAPER TOWEL SACREDNESS

THE ONE

A Single Surface Area

THE MANY

Multiple Surface Areas -- More Absorbant
Generates
New Possibilities
New Learning
New Information
And
Emergence

Of course, this is a physical metaphor. The Sacred isn't really a cosmic paper towel. But the principle is an important one. Differences generate creativity, and differences arise from boundaries and thresholds—i.e. things that separate. These differences arise from sacredness expressing as diverse individualities, each a center in its own right with unique characteristics and contributions to make, each its own star as we saw in the last chapter.

However, the role of individuality, particularly in the incarnate, embodied state that we experience as physical persons, has another important function. It becomes a "Grail" or sacred vessel for experiencing the nature and activity of the Sacred.

We all know the challenge of being with people we don't like or with whom we have little affinity. We've all had the experience of being in a room with strangers who are very different from ourselves and struggling to open a conversation, much less develop a liking and sense of camaraderie with them. We may have little in common with our co-workers on a job, and at times even members of our own family can feel alien to us. Yet, often we have to make an effort to overcome these differences and find common ground so that collaboration is possible. On those occasions when we do overcome the boundaries between ourselves and another person of very different temperament, background and personality and form a friendship, we can feel the power of this accomplishment. While all love and good feeling is precious, the love born out of mastering differences can feel deeper and sweeter than the love that is there just because the other person is like us and we have an automatic resonance together.

It is this ability to create and experience collaboration, friendship, and especially love when the conditions between ourselves and another are so different that makes life in the physical world so valuable and important to the soul. It has been my experience in working with non-physical colleagues and states of being that for the soul, affinity and resonance act much the way space and distance do for us as physical persons. Two souls in resonance will naturally share the same space and be easily accessible to each other. Two souls who are not in resonance will be in different spaces; interaction between them requires intention and an act of will, and even then it may not be easy if their native vibrational states are very different. So, to summon up some metaphors, the soul lives in a world in which like really does attract like, and birds *will* flock together with those of identical feathers.

In such a world, love comes easily and communication is facilitated by an affinity that allows for a sharing of minds and hearts. A sense of connection, of wholeness, even of oneness, is the natural state.

As we know, life in the physical world is very different. Here, people are thrown together and must live and work together whether there's any liking or resonance between them or not. Here we encounter differences much more readily and easily than is the case in many of the subtle worlds; we don't have to think about it or make an effort to overcome the boundaries created by differences in resonance and energy. Something as simple as riding a bus or an airplane finds us crowded together with people whether we all have an affinity or not.

This obviously creates conditions for conflict and misunderstanding, but it also creates conditions in which the soul can understand love more deeply and can develop an *intention to love* that may not be required when in its non-physical state.

Such an intention to love is an essential part of the activity of sacredness. It is one of the ways the sacred fire burns. God, we might say, loves with an intensity and an intention that transcends any barriers, boundaries or differences in order to hold the entire cosmos in all its infinite diversity in a loving embrace. But such intensity and intention is generally not a necessity for the soul on its own level where love flows as naturally and easily as breathing. Love is the sea in which the soul swims, but this doesn't necessarily deepen the soul's understanding and appreciation of this love. Jesus said for us to love our enemies but in the realm of the soul, there are no enemies. How, then, can the soul learn this kind of love that can go beyond oneself to embrace another who sees himself as our enemy?

In the incarnate world, though, we can feel separated from love. It's not automatically all around us; it doesn't automatically spring into being between us and another. To know love, to experience love, we have to discover how to deliberately, consciously, and intentionally understand and transcend barriers to that love. We have to journey into the beingness of love in ways the soul does not.

This is a powerful gift, for through the opportunity that incarnated individuality provides, the soul discovers more deeply than ever what it means to be sacred. The soul can *practice* love and in so doing, deepen its capacity to *be* love.

When we understand this, we realize that as incarnate individuals, we play an important role in the expression of sacredness. To use the images from the last chapter, in the "Oneness state", love simply is, but in the incarnate state in the world of separation and diversity, love has to manifest. That is, it has to be expressed as an activity, not simply enjoyed as a state of being. This gives us an opportunity through our very differences to know what it means to love, not simply as an emotion of affection and caring but as the very glue that holds the cosmos together and fosters its wholeness and unfoldment. Love becomes oneness made visible in the paper towel universe.

This is the power of such a universe. By expanding the "surface area" of sacredness, the phenomenon of individuality allows for both learning *and* the generation of new knowledge and the deepening and expression of sacredness in the form of intentional acts of love beyond what would be possible or needed if there were only Oneness. Though challenging, separation is the doorway through which we can discover the nature of the generative, sacred Mystery from which both the One and the Many emerge.

EXERCISE FOR CHAPTER TWO

Reflection: Honoring Your Uniqueness

The principle is this: you are a unique individual, and as such, you can see the world, engage with it and contribute to it, in ways that no one else can. This exercise is simply a reflection on this principle.

Reflect on the ways in which you are different from everyone else. Some of these differences will be obvious, such as the genetic pattern manifested in your body. There can be many other surface differences. But you should look deeper and try to see just what qualities, talents, perspectives, and traits enable you to see what others might miss and to offer to life what others cannot. This is an exercise in honoring your uniqueness. This uniqueness doesn't isolate you from others; it just allows you to bring an awareness and a capacity for action to a situation that may add something no one else can give, even though their contributions may be equally important in their own, equally unique, way.

Julia's Commentary

How in my life do I see my individuality as something of value and not as something of pain and or alienation? How do I experience the sacredness of my particularity? In a paper towel universe, my bump is a unique and expansive particle of the Creative Source which deepens the activity of the sacred. But so much in our upbringing can devalue us that we might find it difficult to really know the truth of this.

When I run into something or someone who is different from myself and who challenges me in uncomfortable ways, if I can see that difference as something of value rather than as a threat or discomfort, I can learn to love those differences in myself. Instead of, "Oh, no. I don't want to be around this person, she is such an antithesis to what I am," how about, "Oh wow, there is someone deliciously different from my experience. What a treat to have that to expand my sense of possibility. How can I love this difference? What does it add to my world that I don't have?"

In loving the differences between us we simultaneously allow ourselves to accept the differences in ourselves and expand the active love in the world. A friend of mine recently told me of her experience with a person she encountered who was so different from her that they were both tense and uncomfortable. She thought to herself, "There is nothing I can do or say that will make this person like me. All I can do is extend hospitality and make them comfortable and at ease." Which is what she did. In doing so, she found herself relaxing, the other relaxed, and they were able to enjoy each other in their differences. David has often used the concept of hospitality to convey the sense of a loving universe, that welcoming, openhearted reception of one without judgment of difference. When we extend hospitality, we offer a loving safe space to be oneself, and in creating this loving safe space for others, we inhabit it ourselves.

Another challenge to seeing the value of our individuality is the story we tell ourselves about who we are in the world, what we think and why, and how to keep ourselves safe - our self-talk, so to speak. Usually our self-talk is negative, conditioning what we experience to support what we believe to be true. I may be honored for my expertise but not be able to accept the compliment due to a deep sense of unworthiness that is part of my narrative of who I am. This sense of unworthiness will prevent us from recognizing our incarnational value. Through our self-talk we become so enmeshed in our own stories that we diminish our ability to appreciate the differences that come to us. We become so involved in the story about who we are and what we like that we might not be open to the possibilities of seeing a different point of view. We will only allow through our defenses that which supports our world view and our view of ourselves. But we are all built different, from the subtle variations we inherit genetically to the vastly different socio-cultural and familial characteristics of our life's patterns. Learning to love our own differences begins with loving all those differences around us, each with its own special story. I want to honor my individuality but not become so immersed in my own narrative that I cannot be hospitable to another way of looking at life. Every bump on the paper towel is sacred, not just mine.

CHAPTER THREE:
BEING A STAR

Ever since our distant ancestors dropped out of the trees and stood upright on the vast plains of Africa, we have been oriented around a vertical axis. In the beginning, I'm sure those ancient proto-humans thought of safety as *up*, in the trees, and danger as *down*, on the ground where predators roamed. Out of this very practical assessment of their environment, early humans laid the foundation for our mythic imagination. Is it too far-fetched to suppose that the reason we see heaven as above us and hell as below may be rooted in this primeval exploration of standing upright on the ground?

Whatever the reason, there is no doubt that we privilege vertical thinking. We divide society into higher and lower ranks and try to be "upwardly mobile". We speak of a "higher self" wherein our spiritual nature is located as contrasted with a "lower self" that can obstruct that spirituality with its earthly needs and characteristics. When we're happy, we speak of being "up" while when we're sad or depressed, we complain that we're "down".

Our vertical thinking is reinforced by the fact that life on earth is made possible by the energy that comes from the sun, and the sun is in the sky above us. In a hierarchical view that privileges the vertical, Light descends from higher levels. If we feel ourselves on one of the lowest, if not the lowest, rung of creation here in the physical universe, when we seek the Light, we look up to God or to beings who are on a higher rung or closer to the Center (if not actually at the Center) than we are.

"Have some Light, Bro!"

"Thanks, Lord!"

Incarnational Spirituality asks us to think in new ways. The world and the times demand it. At the very least, we need to learn the worldview of ecology so that we can properly engage the environmental challenges such as climate change that threaten us. Ecology involves thinking horizontally. A rain forest is not "higher" than a desert in value; there is no hierarchy of ecosystems, no rank that says goodness comes from meadows but not from swamps or from the peaks of mountains and not from valleys and canyons. All manner of ecosystems are needed for life to prosper and for the health of the planet, not just one or two. As systems, they interact as collaborators. Vertical thinking can lead us to visualize the world in terms of dominance and submission, the "higher" controlling the "lower". But this is not the way to see the interconnectedness and interdependency of the world. We need to think horizontally, partner to partner, not master to servant.

This is the perspective offered by the "galactic" model of spirituality, one in which all beings are "stars" or sources of Light. It is a horizontal spirituality. It's not that "vertical spirituality" is incorrect and must now be abandoned. Rather it's that we need to complement it with a horizontal perspective as well, one that sees Light and Spirit in the world about us, in the bodies we wear, in the nature around us, even in the very fabric of matter. We need to think in a way that is not confined to either up or down, right or left, back or forward. Spirit is all around, and Light flows in all directions.

Both the sun/satellite and the vertical spirituality ways of looking at things lead us to look for Light elsewhere than in ourselves. Incarnational Spirituality takes a different approach, as we have seen. Using a "Galactic" model in which all beings are "stars" or sources of Light, the relationship changes. We are all generative sources of Light.

"Hey, Look! I've got
Light, too!"

"Cool, Man!
We're both alike!"

I call this individual radiance our *Self-Light*. It is the natural emanation of the incarnational process itself. It is not dependent on the level of a person's spirituality; its presence is not a measure of a soul's evolution.

But what is this Light that emanates from our individuality? Is it just a "pass-through" — a Light that we draw down from our soul and then radiate out to the world? Or is it something else? We can find a clue in how the sun generates its light.

The reason a star gives off light is because the temperature at its core is so hot that nuclear fusion takes place. Hydrogen atoms combine to create Helium atoms, and in the process energy is generated in the form of heat and light.

Something analogous happens as part of the incarnational process. Put simply, the Identity and soul qualities of the world, expressed through various subtle energies (as well as through the physical environment), meet the Identity and creative qualities coming from the soul. These fuse to create an emergent incarnational identity, and in the process the unique energy and radiance of Self-Light is generated for this individual.

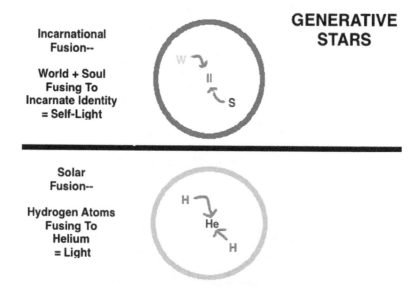

Incarnational Fusion--

World + Soul Fusing To Incarnate Identity = Self-Light

GENERATIVE STARS

Solar Fusion--

Hydrogen Atoms Fusing To Helium = Light

As you might imagine, the physical world and the realm of the soul are two very different manifestations of life, consciousness and energy. There is a "gap"—a differential of energy—between them. Our incarnation and our incarnate identity bridges this gap and joins the two realms together in our own person. This brings something into being that is an emergent phenomenon, that is to say, it didn't exist before and it has properties that may not have been predicted by examining its constituent elements.

Let's use water as an example. A molecule of water is made up of two atoms of hydrogen bonded with one atom of oxygen, hence its chemical notation of H_20. Now hydrogen and oxygen are both gases, but water is a liquid. The wetness and liquidity of water cannot be predicted simply by studying the chemical nature of either hydrogen or oxygen. They are *emergent properties*.

Similarly you can take two minerals, sodium and chloride, either of which is a poison in its natural state, and chemically combine them to produce NaCl or common table salt, a substance essential to physical animal life. The life-giving properties of salt, like those of water, could not be predicted by examination of either sodium or chlorine by itself. They also are emergent properties.

If you mix hydrogen gas and oxygen gas in a room, you don't automatically get water. You just get a mixture of hydrogen and oxygen molecules. To get them to fuse to make water, you have to add energy to break and reform the molecular bonds, a process that in itself also releases energy, often explosively.

A soul that is not in incarnation (that is, it has no physical body) can visit the physical world and to some extent interact energetically with it. When we feel blessed by an invisible, spiritual presence, this is what is happening. But the soul and the world remain separate, just as the hydrogen and oxygen molecules remain separate when you put both gases into a room, and the interaction is limited. However, when a soul incarnates, a very different process ensues (more than just "entering a body" like a driver entering a car). Two different states of life, consciousness, and energy—that of the World soul and that of the human soul—blend and fuse to create a new identity, one with its own emergent properties. This new identity is the incarnate individual and his or her personality.

The soul of the world (which I call "Gaia") and the soul of the human individual are two very different manifestations of life. It takes energy to get them to blend, and in turn, this process releases or generates energy. It's this energy that I call our Self-Light. It is a product, an emanation, of the incarnational process itself.

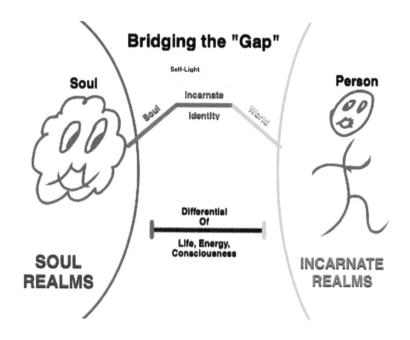

The soul in incarnation is different from the soul that is disincarnate and living on its own level or wavelength of life within the subtle worlds. It can interact with the world from the inside, so to speak, as part of the incarnate realms. This interaction, as we shall see later, goes beyond simply engaging physically with the earthly environment. An incarnation is more than just being in or having a body. The essence of incarnation is that it is a fusion of two different states of life and beingness, one that possesses new, emergent properties and capacities.

One of these properties is that it is generative, like a star. Each of us radiates a Self-Light which is not simply another kind of subtle energy but a true spiritual emanation that nurtures and fosters spiritual life, just as sunlight, the light of our closest star, nurtures and fosters physical life.

Although all individuals radiate this Self-Light, not all individuals do so to the same degree. In the galaxy there are bright stars and dim stars, yet they are still stars. The same process of nuclear fusion is occurring within them however large or small, dim or bright they may be. The same is true for people. Our Self-Light can be obscured by thoughts, emotions, attitudes, and activities, or it can be enhanced, as we shall see in later chapters. But whatever the radiance of our Self-Light may be, it is always there. We are each of us always a generative source, a "star", not a planet.

EXERCISE FOR CHAPTER THREE

Where Stars Meet

- Imagine a spiritual star at the center of the earth. It's a green star radiant with the power of planetary life and the soul of the World, Gaia. Imagine the light from this star rising up through the earth, surrounding you, bathing and nurturing the cells of your body and forming a chalice around you.
- Imagine a spiritual star within the sun in the sky. It's a golden star radiant with the power of your soul. Imagine the light from this star descending from the heavens and pouring into the chalice of earthlight that surrounds you and fills your cells.
- Where the green and golden lights of these two stars meet in you, a new star emerges, a radiant star of Self-Light, born of the blending of the individual and the universal, the planetary and the cosmic, the physical and the spiritual, the soul and the world. This Self-Light surrounds you and fills you, radiating back down deep into the earth and out into space, connecting with the star below you and the star above you. You are a Chalice of Self-Light within a pillar of spiritual energy rising from the earth and descending from the cosmos.
- Take a moment to feel the star of this Self-Light within and around you. It is your connection to the earth, your connection to the cosmos, your connection to your own unique and radiant Self. Take a deep breath, drawing this Light into and throughout your body; breathe out, sending this Light out into your world. Filled with this Light of Self, attuned to heaven and earth, go about your day as a star of blessing.

Julia's Commentary

No matter how evolved we might or might not be, we are still a source of light on earth, a generative star of radiance.

It is easier, in traditional, vertical spiritual orientations, to regard our personal incarnate selves as being without value, something to get beyond and ultimately leave behind as we launch into glorious transcendence. What is above is best and most desired, and what is below is something to get over. Who can resist the charisma and beauty of the soul? Reformatting our thoughts to the recognition that something dynamic is going on here on earth, which is also magical and light-filled, can be difficult. We seem to spend much of our lives fighting with parts of ourselves and comparing ourselves with an ideal which we can never reach.

But I have seen time and again, as an individual grasps that this personal self has a light of its own and is capable of making a contribution to the world in its own right, some part of us gets liberated. We are allowed to appreciate our differences, to celebrate with joy the variety that humanity embraces, to value the richness that all those unique notes add to the song of life. It allows us to create a bridge between the transcendent and our earthly engagement and adds a lightness to where we stand in the world.

Can you be in your environment and recognize that on a spiritual level you have something to offer? You have the wherewithal within you to be a source of spiritual energy or blessing and it is up to you to be aware of, to direct and make use of it. Self-Light is a natural part of our engagement with the world, but becoming aware of it shifts your identity and your sense of yourself. By consciously recognizing and standing in it, you can begin to see yourself as someone who is a source of the blessing and nurturing that spirit provides. This light lies as a potential within us always, but our intent makes it brighter - energizes, awakens and sets it into motion such that it is a gift to the community, and you become a source of spiritual presence in the environment of the world.

CHAPTER FOUR:
SOVEREIGNTY

Incarnation is like an alchemical process. Two different elements, Soul and World, are brought together and out of their combination and blending, something new emerges: an incarnate identity.

THE ALCHEMY OF SELF-LIGHT

But what is it that enables Soul and World to blend in this way, becoming one? What enables the crossing of the "gap" — the differential of life, consciousness, and energy — that we talked about in the last chapter? There are two forces at work here: Sovereignty and Love. We'll talk about love in the next chapter. First, I want to define what I mean by Sovereignty.

SOVEREIGNTY

Over the years, in David's classes, I have come to understand sovereignty to refer to the self's innate capacity for integrity and wholeness up and down, over and across, and throughout the various domains of being in which we participate and from which we draw our

*substance and our form. The creative process that brings each person
into existence traverses heights and depths of reality that range from
the most expansive, luminous, and abstract realms beyond the human
to the most material, obdurate, and concrete matter close at hand,
accumulating and joining together aspects of them all. Throughout
this process, and within each person, it is sovereignty, like Ariadne's
thread, that connects the levels to one another and imparts a resonance
of identity to the whole.*

---Jim Hembree

This quote is from a chapter in a new anthology to be published
by Lorian Press. Called *The Voices of Incarnational Spirituality*, it's a
collection of articles written by people all over the world describing
their experiences as they have been making Incarnational Spirituality
their daily practice. Here Jim expresses as clearly as I have ever done
the nature of that which holds our incarnations in coherency and
balance, a quality I call *Sovereignty*.

Sovereignty is our capacity to be self-governing. It's a measure
of our ability to "be ourselves" and to express our will and identity in
the world. But this capacity comes from Sovereignty's deeper nature.
It is the link between the Identity of the Soul and our personality. It is
the sense of "I AM", and as such, it is the energetic "spine" or "axis"
around which the incarnational identity can form and integrate as
it develops coherency and wholeness. In this sense, Sovereignty is
our personal, incarnational organizing principle.

A pile of logs and a log cabin are both "systems" but one is
organized and the other is not (at least not by human standards). A
Home Depot warehouse store has everything I need to build a house.
In it I will find row upon row of lumber, carpentry supplies, plumbing
fixtures, lighting and electrical supplies, kitchen sinks, refrigerators,
washing machines and dryers, furnaces, and so on. Yet sitting in the
warehouse, they do not form a home. They represent a potential.

Sovereignty is like the vision and plan I have for the home I
would like to build. My home will have all the same materials that I
find at Home Depot, but they will be organized into new relationships
and partnerships with each other according to my vision. When I

visit the warehouse to select what I'll need, it's like the Soul engaging with what I call the *Incarnate Realms* (all the mental, emotional, physical, energetic, and spiritual content that makes up the earth) to begin attracting what it will need for its new incarnation. When Home Depot delivers everything I've selected, it comes as a jumble of stuff, lumber here, sinks there, plumbing over there, electrical wires here, and so on. It's my vision, my energy, my identity, my love that assembles all this material and turns it into a house and then into a home. What I call Sovereignty is the dynamic, alchemical, integrating, co-creating relationship I form with all the material from Home Depot that enables it to transform from "stuff" to "home".

Sovereignty and Identity

Sovereignty is like the Soul's "executive officer" within the complexity of connections that make up the Soul's relationship with the World. It ensures that amidst all these connections, each pulling in its own way, the Soul's Identity is paramount and acts as the synthesizing and organizing agency. Sovereignty provides the energetic link between the Soul's consciousness and Identity and all its activity and development within the Incarnate Realms.

If I were to use the metaphor of writing a novel, then Sovereignty is the core idea and felt sense of the story, the emotional and mental impact that I wish a reader to take away from having read it. When I write stories, this core idea is not always something I can put into words; it's more like the feeling tone which the story will "incarnate" in the world.

In writing a story, many different ideas will come to me, ideas for characters, plot lines, scenes, settings, relationships and connections within the story, and so on. I may find many of these ideas attractive, but the ones I choose will ultimately be the ones that can resonate with the story's felt sense and core purpose. They are the ones that align with and further the story's core identity. They are the ones that align with the story's Sovereignty.

Sovereignty and Boundaries

Sovereignty creates and maintains our boundaries. Our

boundaries shape and form the space within which our Sovereignty is the organizing principle, and that organizing principle in turn helps define and strengthen the boundaries. To "stand in your Sovereignty" is also to "stand in your boundaries".

Boundaries establish a space within which sovereignty can operate without interference. If I want to do some work at my desk, I clear a space within which that work can take place. I establish the area of my work. Inside this area, I can put whatever papers, pencils, books, files, and so forth that I wish, and I can organize and process them as I wish. Our skin is a physical example of a boundary. But we have psychological, energetic, and spiritual boundaries as well, all of which define where our sovereignty operates in those particular domains.

Boundaries do not need to be walls, all stiff and hard and resistant. Ideally, they are like interfaces or membranes: fluid, dynamic, interactive, and configurable. They exist not only to define and protect an area of sovereignty but to establish "betweenness" by defining the capacities and rules for interaction, engagement, connection, and co-creativity. Boundaries provide a meeting ground between different entities, and their nature establishes how that meeting may take place and what can happen.

When boundaries are trespassed or breached, sovereignty is diminished. Integrity, coherency, and wholeness may be compromised or lost. Identity is infringed. We become less capable.

Boundaries do more than just define and protect. The space they create is also a holding space. So, using the illustration of clearing a space on my desk, that space can now hold whatever activity I wish to perform on my desk.

But this is a passive sense of holding. The holding that Sovereignty and boundaries enable is more active; the defined, sovereign space interacts with what is within it according to the characteristics of the boundaries, the sovereignty, and the identity that form it.

Thus my novel is defined by the feeling and intellectual tone I wish it to have (its identity) and by the specific genre characteristics I've chosen to use to tell the story (its boundary; for instance, it's a science fiction story and not a real-life romance or a fantasy). These two establish the Sovereignty of the story and create a "literary space" that will hold the contents of the story. But within this space, characters, plot lines, settings, and so forth can all interact both with each other and with the characteristics of the space itself (i.e. the overall intent of the novel) as determined by its Sovereignty. I may find the story "writing itself" as ideas emerge out of this interaction, ideas that I may not have foreseen or anticipated.

This happens in incarnation, too. The Soul has its Identity and through its intent establishes the boundaries of the new life-to-be, thus creating an energy and presence of Sovereignty with which it engages the world. This Sovereignty becomes the "spine" (or the felt sense of the incarnation's essence) around which all the connections with the Incarnate Realms can form. This in turn creates and holds a space that can both hold the incarnating energy and presence of the Soul and allow the emergence of a particular incarnational identity. In a way, the incarnation begins to "write itself" within this spiritual, subtle, energetic, psychological, physical, and environmental space.

Sovereignty as a Universal Principle

Although each of us has his or her unique Sovereignty, Sovereignty itself is a "non-local" and transpersonal phenomenon. This means that as a force that preserves and supports the integrity and wholeness of incarnation and the incarnational process, it is everywhere present. Rocks have their Sovereignty, trees have their Sovereignty, birds have their Sovereignty, bears and kittens have their Sovereignty, and, of course, all people do. Gaia itself has its planetary Sovereignty. And the paradox is that it's all the same principle of Sovereignty in action. Which means that I can't diminish your Sovereignty without diminishing my own. It's like saying I can't pollute the air you breathe without polluting my air as well.

Nearly forty-six years ago, on March 31, 1968, Dr. Martin Luther King, Jr. gave a talk at the National Cathedral in Washington, D.C. in which he said among other things,

We are tied together in the single garment of destiny, caught in an inescapable network of mutuality. And whatever affects one directly affects all indirectly. For some strange reason I can never be what I ought to be until you are what you ought to be. And you can never be what you ought to be until I am what I ought to be. This is the way God's universe is made; this is the way it is structured.

This is exactly how Sovereignty operates. It's not an "I-can-do-my-own-thing" dominion over others or over the world. It's an inner dominion or organization that grows in strength as others are enabled to know and express their Sovereignty as well.

This may seem strange. What happens if my Sovereignty conflicts with yours? Doesn't this lead to conflict? But to think this way is to misunderstand the nature of Sovereignty and the fields that emerge around it. To be self-governing, I don't have to be other-governing. If I enter into a relationship or connection with another, then a space of "mutuality", to use Dr. King's lovely word, opens between us, and that space has its own Sovereignty, too, a Sovereignty that is not a force of dominion over us but a force of clarity, integration, coherency, and wholeness between us.

We are constantly creating fields of interaction and potential wholeness between ourselves and everything within the world around us. Sovereignty isn't a force of dominion and control through these interactions; it's a force of love, wholeness, and emergence.

EXERCISE FOR CHAPTER FOUR

Standing

This is a core exercise in the practice of Incarnational Spirituality. It is a way of attuning to Sovereignty and to the uniqueness, strength and presence of your individuality.

As you do this exercise and move up the different levels from the physical to the spiritual, be aware of an axis of power, energy and identity rising up within you, connecting all these levels together. Like an inner spine, this is a quality of energy and presence that I call Sovereignty. What you are looking for is the felt sense of this energy and identity within you.

Physical:

The physical action of this exercise is simple. From a sitting position, you simply stand up. Be aware of the physical sensation and felt sense of standing. Feel the work of your body, the power of balance that keeps you upright. If you are already standing, become aware that you are standing and be mindful of the felt sense of standing. In standing you are asserting your physical power to rise up against the power of gravity that would pull you down. You are celebrating your strength. If you are physically unable to stand, you can still assume an inner attitude of standing, perhaps simply by straightening your spine as much as possible.

Emotional:

Feel the power of being upright. Feel how standing singles you out and expresses your individuality and sovereignty. You stand for what you believe, you stand up to be counted. Standing proclaims that you are here. Standing says you are ready to make choices and decisions. Feel the strength and presence of your identity and sovereignty.

Mental:

Celebrate your humanness. You are an upright being. You emerge from the mass of nature, from the vegetative and animal states into a realm of thinking and imagining. In standing, your hands are released from providing locomotion. Feel the freedom of your hands that don't have to support you but can now be used to create, manipulate, touch, and express your thoughts, your imagination, and your sovereignty.

Magical (Energetic):
When you stand, your spine becomes a magical staff, the axis mundi and center of your personal world, generating the field that embraces you. The spine is the traditional wizard's staff along which spiritual power flows and the centers of energy sing in resonance with the cosmos. Feel your energy field coming into alignment with the stars above, the earth below, and the environment around you. Feel your energy aligning with the sovereignty of all beings above, below, and around.

Spiritual:
Standing, you are the incarnate link between heaven and earth. Your energy rises into the sky and descends into the earth. Light descends and ascends, swirling along your spine in a marriage of matter and spirit. This energy is both personal and transpersonal, giving birth to something new, something human, individual and unique. Feel the magic and energy of your sovereignty that connects soul to person, the higher-order consciousness with the consciousness of the incarnate realms. Feel the will that emerges from this connection, the spiritual presence that blends heaven and earth, aligning with the Sovereignty of creation as it manifests through you.

In doing this exercise of Standing, physically stand if you are able. If you are not able to do so, then be as upright as you can be in your physical situation and in your imagination, "stand" mentally and emotionally. The important thing is to have the felt sense of standing and being upright even if you are physically unable to do so. As you do so, work through these levels of sensation, feeling, thought, energy, and spirit, appreciating the power, the freedom, and the presence emerging within you from the simple act of standing. All of these manifest your unique Identity and Sovereignty, connecting and aligning you with all levels of your being, providing an axis around which integration and coherency can occur, creating wholeness and establishing your capacity for agency and self-governance.

Julia's Commentary

Sovereignty is our capacity to be self-governing. It's a measure of our ability to "be ourselves" and to express our will and identity in the world. It is the link between the Identity of the Soul and our personality.
(David Spangler)

The constellation of concepts and practices represented by the standing exercise are to me at the core of Incarnational Spirituality. If I can experience myself as a generative source of spiritual substance standing on a sacred earth I have the keys to participating here and now with a gifting universe in which I too am a gift. Who could ask for more?
(Jeremy Berg)

For many of us, it is not hard to get a clear sense of our sovereignty when we look back on key life events. There are times in everyone's life when we feel strong, aligned with something powerful and affirming inside us. For some, this happens out in nature, for others it might be in a time of accomplishment or spiritual refreshment. But those times don't always stick around. That strong center gets overpowered by our interactions with life's challenges or everyday encounters with the differences of others. (They may not see how magnificent we are!) So that sense of sovereignty shifts and wavers. And we can encounter situations which throw us off balance causing us to lose our standing center. It is a challenge to stand strong in ourselves and still be able to be receptive to others in order to partner with them. Sensitive people may try to understand and blend with their world by 'erasing' the boundaries between themselves and others, seeking to be one. But boundaries are important to our incarnational integrity, and there is a way to stand in the integrity of ourselves and still be able to deeply connect with our world. Opening our hearts does not mean we lose our individuality.

Practicing the Standing exercise helps us be able to sustain that center in the face of changing circumstances. Our recognition of our sense of sovereignty and how and when we lose that center is a huge part of being able to find it again. That is why practicing is important

—getting the groove laid down so the pattern is more accessible.

But it is also part of Sovereignty to be able to blend with others from that center. Not losing our boundaries, but being able to stand in the center of our identities and allow flow around us. Strong barriers which separate us might be helpful or necessary at first, but being able to merge and flow with others is also part of communication and partnership. So how do we stand in the river of life, part of the flow, and yet be a clear voice of ourselves?

The Standing Exercise, which brings into focus and practice the sense memory of Sovereignty, anchors that state in my cells, in my body sense, in my feeling self, in my mind and intent. It connects me with my world, but also connects me with my larger self in the subtle worlds. So this is a practice of bringing your whole self together, standing here on the earth. Your expression here is still shaped and colored by the specific patterns within you created by your personality, history and heredity, but you will not lose your ability to stand in yourself with alignment to the wholeness of you.

This is why paying attention to loving your self, your body, your emotions, and your personal identity in this life is essential to standing in Sovereignty. If you diminish any part of yourself, you can't hold sovereignty when that part shows up. So if it doesn't hold but waivers and wobbles in the face of life's currents, what in you is being disregarded or devalued? How can you name that part and include it in the loving? How can you value that part? What does that part give you that is an asset? It might be a hurt part needing healing and realignment, or it might be a part that actually is a strength from another perspective.

Suppose I am with my family for the holidays (a common time for losing center), and old patterns from childhood arise to make me wobble. I can moan and say to myself "there I go again. I can never be who I am with these people". Or I can notice the wobble. Say hello to the little me who has these habits and memories. Love little me from my grown up center and from that place where I know how to stand in my Sovereignty. Having practiced, it is a familiar place. Now, here I am losing my sense of Sovereignty with my family, and I can STAND, remind myself of who I know myself to be in a larger context, and hit reset. I can then love little me and let all the strain of past stuff flow away. I can approach this moment as new, seeing those around me as they are without projections from my memories and habits. Our past is an important part of what makes us who we are in the present. It is part of our wholeness and part of our sovereignty as it provides the foundations of where we stand upon the earth. In my sovereignty, I can accept all those parts of my past as essential building blocks of who I am in the present, and I can love the gifts I have gained from them.

I have practiced standing in line at the grocery checkout. I have practiced while walking for my exercise. I have practiced when making may bed in the morning, or even when I have been doing something I dislike. Any time you think of it, STAND. Remember that feeling in your body, in your soul, in your Self. Hold that and move out from that into your activity.

Our protective barriers can be helpful to hold our individuality and identity when we feel too permeable. Once we are settled in the strength of our Sovereignty, we don't get thrown off so easily, and we no longer need the protection of impermeable boundaries which can isolate us. We can use radiant boundaries instead. For instance, if I go into the mall simply feeling open to others, I can get overwhelmed by all the different voices there. If I go into the mall standing in my deep Self, radiating the love that is there, I can touch the sacredness within all that the mall is and all who are within it, washing them in love, blessing them. Then I find they don't invade me and throw me off center. It is much easier to navigate this complex field of beings without a need to protect myself from harm. The field of loving becomes a protection, and I can still blend as I go. If I bump into a grumpy person, because I am not just in receiving mode taking in the energies I encounter, but am in gifting mode, the grumpiness does not negatively impact me. In fact, through standing in that field of love and radiance, I just might be able to give that grumpy person a lift, helping a fellow traveler to shift their energy for a time.

Hopefully, as we get more practiced at standing in our Sovereignty, we can relax the protective barriers we have set in order to hold our identity. We stand as a rock in the flow, without fear of losing ourselves, and we can enter into communion with our world and those beings within it. From this, partnership and collaboration come more easily.

CHAPTER FIVE:
LOVE

Incarnation is like an alchemical process. Two different elements, Soul and World, are brought together and out of their combination and blending, something new emerges: an incarnate identity.

But what is it that enables Soul and World to blend in this way? What enables the crossing of the "gap"—the differential of life, consciousness, and energy—that we talked about in the last chapter? As I said there, there are two forces at work here: Sovereignty and Love. We've talked about Sovereignty. Now let's talk about love.

THE ALCHEMY OF INCARNATION

THE IDENTITY OF GAIA (THE WORLD)

The Incarnational Fire

The fundamental love that enables the incarnational process is the love of the Soul for the World. If I think of the various elements of energy, life, and consciousness that make up the Earth as kindling, then this love is like a spark of soul that lands in its midst, creating the alchemical "fire" that produces an incarnate self and the Light that emanates from it. At the earliest point in our incarnational history, we are each "born" from an act of love within the soul.

LOVING THE WORLD

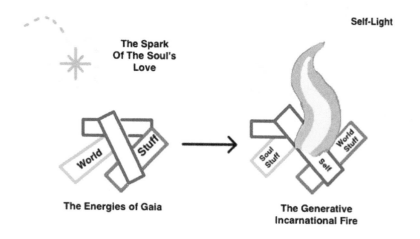

This alchemy takes place at a deep level of our being, generally beyond the reach of our conscious mind. However, while I don't control the chemical processes of combustion that turn the wood of a campfire into its various components, I can blow on the fire to make it burn hotter and brighter. In an analogous way, through consciously loving myself and the world around me, I can enhance the presence and activity of this alchemical love within myself.

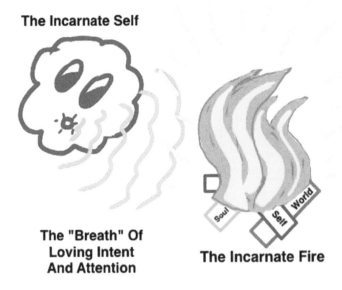

The Incarnate Self

The "Breath" Of Loving Intent And Attention

The Incarnate Fire

So how do we love? How do we participate in this inner fire, enhancing through our loving intent and attention the Self-Light we radiate and the blessings we offer the world around us?

The Spectrum of Love

Most spiritual practices of which I am aware share in common an injunction to love. In the Christian tradition, for example, we are told to "love our neighbors" and to love those who hurt or misuse us. Other religions and philosophies have similar doctrines. There is no question that when we are able to do this, transformations and miracles take place. It's the doing of it that's the challenge.

Not that it's hard to be loving in the abstract. I can love people all day long when I'm by myself. It's when I meet other folks that the challenge begins. As Linus, the blanket-toting little philosopher in Charles Schulz's comic strip *Peanuts*, says, "I love humanity. It's people I can't stand."

When we think of love, we think of an emotion that manifests warmth, attraction, acceptance, even approval and affection. It is an emotion—and an action—that connects us in some manner. We may think of love as bonding, like a kind of psychological or spiritual glue. But we all know that we meet people with whom we don't wish to bond and encounter situations with which we don't want to be connected; at such times, we don't feel acceptance, attraction, or approval, much less warmth and affection. How, then, to fulfill the call to love?

Part of the problem is that we have an image of what love is supposed to be like, particularly unconditional love. When we don't live up to that particular image, we think of ourselves as unloving. It's like saying that a light bulb is either on or off, either glowing or not. But some lights have a dimmer switch that allows them to shine with varying degrees of intensity from very bright to hardly noticeable but not altogether off. Love is like that. It also exists along a spectrum. It has stages, too, from dim to bright.

Before discussing these stages, though, let me offer my definition of love. After all, the quality of light that a bulb gives off is the same however the dimmer switch is set. Dim light is essentially no different from bright light; both are comprised of photons in motion. In an analogous way, there is a quality to love that is the same wherever the expression of it is along this spectrum; there is an "essence of love." What is that?

We hear the phrase that love is about the "ties that bind." Actually, love is about the connections that give freedom and allow individuals to know and stand in their own uniqueness and Sovereignty. This quality of love isn't about attraction, acceptance, approval, or even affection. Rather, it is a way of seeing and holding another's individuality and identity within the life of the Sacred. It unites both giver and receiver with the larger wholeness of creation and sacredness. It is a gift of freedom, not a form of bondage.

Love is freeing, not binding, but it *is* an act that empowers connection: connection with oneself, connection with others, connection with the world, connection with possibility and potential, connection with the Sacred. This connection is one in which each participant can thrive and unfold in safety within themselves, in their relationships, and in what they offer to the world. It is a partnering connection in which each is a gift to the other demanding nothing in return. As such, love reveals and expresses the ultimate Gift through which the Sacred gives of itself that the universe may exist and unfold. Each act of love replicates to some degree that primal Gift.

With this in mind, we can now look at different degrees of loving, understanding that each of them offers this nourishment in one way or another.

The first stage of love is *perception.* At one level this is as basic as seeing that another exists at all. By perceiving, I am drawing that person into the field of my consciousness and awareness. I am saying inwardly, "I'm not shutting my eyes on you." I may not like the person or what he or she does or stands for, but as an act of love, I'm not blanking them out and saying he or she doesn't exist.

This act of seeing goes beyond a simple perception that someone or something is there. It is an act of deliberate, mindful awareness of the unique characteristics of the person who is seen. You are drawing them out of the background smear of perception, out of the abstraction of "humanity," and seeing them as a specific person. You may not like them. You don't have to like them. You may wish them to go away or for you to go away so that you have nothing to do with each other. At this stage of love, that's ok. But if you do move away from each other, you do so having seen the other.

To see another is the opposite of ignoring the other. You are not treating the other as if he or she were not there at all, as if, like Cellophane Man in the musical *Chicago,* this person had no existence worth noting. You may not like that existence, but you are seeing it. If love is a way of valuing someone or something, you have to see that a person or thing is there before any value can be assigned.

When someone says to me, "I just can't love this person," my response may be to say, "Well, don't try to be loving. Be perceptive." Taking the time and making the effort to see another may be the step that begins to open the heart and thus turn up the dimmer switch on your lovingness.

A second stage is *acknowledgement.* This is very similar to perceiving, and the two can blend into each other, but I find it helpful to distinguish between them. To perceive is to say, "You exist." To acknowledge is to say, "You have the right to exist. I see that you

49

are here in the world with me and you have a right to be here in the world with me."

We all see things in the world that we feel don't have a right to be here or wish were not here. When we see someone behaving in violent, abusive, and hurtful ways, we are right to say we don't want that kind of behavior to exist. But this is different from saying we don't wish the person to exist. If someone exists, he or she has the possibility of changing and transforming. If we take that existence away, no change is possible. My earlier definition of love includes connection with possibility. I don't have to accept, like, approve of, or otherwise endorse negative behavior, but love acknowledges and empowers connection to possibility—the possibility of change, redemption, growth, and blessing. Love in the form of simple acknowledgement holds forth and nourishes the potential for this possibility.

A third stage is what I call *honoring*. Honoring is saying, "You have a right to exist and to be different from me." Honoring is a form of perception and acknowledgement, but one that goes a bit further. Honoring as I use the term is not the same as either liking or approving, much less affection. It is a further form of perception and acknowledgement, but this time one that values and accepts differences.

This is where love as we usually think of it begins to show itself, for when we can acknowledge and accept differences, we are coming to where we can value the individuality of the other, which is the basis of a healthy loving relationship. Love is all about valuing and nourishing a person's uniqueness, enabling that individuality to thrive and discover itself as well as enabling it to find appropriate ways of connecting to the rest of the world. If I deny you the ways in which you are different from me and I try to change you to be more like me, then I am not loving you in an honoring manner. I am denying you your individuality.

There is nothing about honoring that prohibits anyone from changing in order to better connect with another; it simply says that this is not necessary in order to be loved.

From honor grows *appreciation*. This is closer to the kind

of affection and acceptance we often think of as love, though I can
certainly appreciate someone without particularly liking him or her.
I think of appreciation as being open to knowing you and through
that knowing, valuing you. Appreciation in this context for me
is saying, "I see you, you exist, you have a right to exist and to be
different from me, and I am open to going past those differences to
knowing you as you are." And as I do come to know you, one effect
is that ways can emerge in which our differences can work together
and become co-creative.

Appreciation is a recognition of the place another person or an
object occupies in an interconnected cosmos, their participation in a
larger ecology of being. I can appreciate the person or object and be
grateful for what they offer me or do for me, but in fact, this stage
of loving goes beyond this, valuable as such gratefulness can be.
Appreciation is also the act of evaluating something, not judging it but
being aware of its qualities and how it connects to the world around
it. In a way, to appreciate is to *apprehend* in the sense of gaining or
taking in deeper knowledge about something by perceiving it more
clearly and fully.

Appreciation leads into a sense of **caring**. Now I not only
appreciate that which I love, I also feel a sense of participation in
its well-being and perhaps even its destiny. I feel invested to some
degree in what happens to the object of my love. I want to do
what I can to help it find its own unique wholeness, identity, and
fulfillment.

Out of this caring can develop **connectedness**, a sense of bonding
or at least a deeper involvement with the object of my love. I can
feel how my life and that of the object of my love are entwined in
some manner, making us valuable to each other. I begin to feel the
other as part of me.

Caring and a sense of connectedness can then lead to **affection**,
a resonance of the heart and a sense of kinship. Such affection brings
with it a desire for the highest good of that which I love. It's a deeper
sense of bonding and often brings with it a wish to be involved in
some manner with the object of my affection. More than a simple
sense of connection, through affection I want the object of my love to

51

be part of my life, and I wish to be part of its existence as well.

Beyond affection are even deeper and more intimate forms of love in which we feel increasingly one with our beloved as if we are partners in co-creating a larger whole. What these forms may be depends on the individuals and the situation involved as they will unfold out of the uniqueness of the participants.

Moving through this sequence can happen very quickly, or it can be a slow process (and you might identify other stages that I haven't thought of that are meaningful to you). As I describe in my book *Apprenticed to Spirit*, I was once given an assignment by my mentor John to learn to love a man whom I had seen on TV and who had committed a particularly heinous crime. It literally took me months to accomplish this. For a long time, the best I could do was to simply acknowledge the existence of this man and grant him a right to share the universe with me! Eventually, though, I was able to move to a place of truly loving and caring for this individual as a fellow child of God.

When we are told to love as a spiritual discipline or action, we usually think we need to leap directly to a sense of affection and deep caring for the object of our loving. But sometimes it's very hard to do this. How do I bring myself to love and open my heart to someone like Hitler or a child molester or a serial killer? Realizing that love is a spectrum that runs from acknowledgement to affection and beyond has been very helpful for me. If I can't manage the "high end" of this spectrum in a particular circumstance, I don't have to give up and say, "I just can't love in this circumstance." I can find a place on this spectrum where I can start out and then I can work up from there.

We can be loving in a variety of ways that don't always look like the stereotypical images of "spiritual love" or "unconditional love" but which still embody the essence of the Sacred's primal gift. Of course we may strive for that kind of unconditional and compassionate love that we imagine is the province of saints, adepts and spiritual masters of one kind or another. But if love is a spectrum, then we don't have to have the dimmer switch set to "brightest" in order to express love, and that means we don't have to beat ourselves up, consider ourselves unworthy, or sit in judgment on our spiritual nature if the best we can muster is "well, ok, I see you and acknowledge that you exist and have a right to do so." It is unloving to ourselves to beat ourselves up for our failure to be saintly!

What I have experienced over the years is that if I accept that "dim love" is better than no love at all, it doesn't leave me satisfied with that dimness but it doesn't leave me critical of my performance either. I accept what I can offer in a particular situation to a particular person in the moment, and that acceptance becomes a seed in my heart from which a fuller expression of love can grow.

The fact is that even mustering the effort and energy to perceive, to acknowledge, to honor, and to appreciate can be challenging and can exercise our "love-muscles" and contribute to opening our hearts more fully. We all start somewhere. Even winners of multiple Olympic gold medals started by crawling.

In short, as we turn the "dimmer switch of love" up towards increasing "brightness," we shorten the psychological and spiritual distance between ourselves and the person (or object) we are considering. We begin with "I see you but I don't necessarily want to know you or have anything to do with you," and move towards, "I appreciate you and am open to knowing you and having something to do with you." We are moving increasingly towards the kind of manifestation and relationships that we think of when we think of love.

I'd like to end with a thought about unconditional love. This is a term that is much used in spiritual circles and held up as our objective. We are enjoined to learn to love unconditionally. But I think this term can be misleading. What I think people who use this term are really trying to say is that we want to love without reservation, without holding back or making our love dependent on something external to ourselves.

The phrase "unconditional love," on the other hand, can be interpreted to mean "love that ignores and is not bound by conditions" and thus is the same for all people in all situations. But the fact is that we are conditioned beings; we embody specificity and particularity, not universality. To this end, love can be without reservation but it still needs to pay attention to conditions and configure itself appropriately.

If I have two friends, and one enjoys reading while the other enjoys playing games, I may love both unreservedly, but in expressing my love, I want to get the one a book while giving the other a board game. In short, I am aware of and honoring the specifics—the conditions—of their lives. To do otherwise is really not to be loving at all. I can say that it doesn't matter what I give them as it's the loving thought that counts, but if I took the time and energy to see them, acknowledge them, honor them, and appreciate them, I would understand that it's the differences that count as well. If I ignore the conditions of their lives that make them different, how can I say I really know and love them?

This is particularly true when it comes to honoring and respecting boundaries, our own and those of others. Sometimes the loving act is to leave conditions as they are, to maintain our boundaries and our separateness, and to respect the separateness of others. Not all things are meant to be connected in a particular way at a particular time and place. The loving act may be to recognize this.Love, to be effective and appropriate, is often bound by conditions, but it can be unreserved as well. I do not have to limit my love in order to shape its expression to the limits and conditions I find around me. I find this all the time in dealing with subtle beings from the higher orders of spiritual life. Such beings are pure embodiments of love, yet they do not come blasting in to my life, blinding me with their radiance and overwhelming me with their presence and their love. They pay attention to who I am and where I am in my spiritual development. They are respectful of my boundaries and limitations. They give me what I can endure and integrate and perhaps just enough more that I will stretch and grow. They are unreserved in their loving, but they are not unconditional.

EXERCISES FOR CHAPTER FIVE

Loving Perception

<u>Introduction:</u>

This exercise is based on exploring and experiencing different stages along the spectrum of love:

- Perception
- Acknowledgement
- Honoring
- Appreciation
- Caring
- Connection
- Affection

In these exercises, as with anything dealing with love, remember that the function of love is to enhance freedom and the holopoietic impulse. Love is not the tying of a cord of energy around someone or something to bind them to you in some way but an act of blessing that sees them standing in their Sovereignty and freedom and able to respond freely from their own wholeness.

<u>The Exercise, Part 1:</u>

Take an object and place it before you. Begin with just seeing it, looking it over and getting a sense of its physical shape and appearance, an awareness of how the object manifests in the physical world. Then when you feel ready, move on to expressing love through Acknowledgement, then through Honoring, Appreciation, Caring, Connection, and Affection, moving "up" the levels of loving as far as you can, each level taking you deeper and closer into communion and connection with your object.

What differences do you feel as you do this? What connection do you feel with your object as you do this? What changes do you feel in yourself? As your love for this object of perception deepens and expands, does its inner nature become more alive within you?

When you've gone as far as you wish, or when you feel restless and tired, express your gratitude to the object and set it aside, going about your normal day.

The Exercise, Part 2:

As you go through your day, encountering people and things, note in passing where on the spectrum of love your response or relationship to them falls. If you have an opportunity and can do so appropriately without harm to anyone, see if you can "turn the dimmer switch" to move to the next higher level of loving. What is this like?

The Touch of Love

- Fill yourself with a felt sense of lovingness. You might imagine, for instance, your heart overflowing with love or your spine glowing with love. You might use one of the exercises given above for enhancing your transpersonal "circulation".
- Feel this love flowing out from the core of your being, down your arms and into your hands. Feel this love pooling in your fingertips.
- Reach out and touch something. As you do so, feel the love in your fingertips overflowing. In this Touch of Love, you do not take anything into yourself. You do not really project it into anything, either. You simply let it pool in your fingertips and overflow, allowing that which you touch to absorb it in its own way.
- As love flows through your touch, it also stirs and flows and circulates through your own being, bring love to all parts of yourself just as you are bringing it to the things you touch.
- Touch as many things as you wish. When you feel finished, just remove your fingers and allow the love to be absorbed into all parts of your body.

We touch each other's incarnations all the time. The energies we project to each other, the way we think of each other, the feelings we surround others with, the looks we give, the tones of voice, the words we use: all these are touches. But are they touches that help us to incarnate and help the incarnation of another, or do they hinder and obstruct? That is what only we can determine.

David Spangler

Julia's Commentary

*We touch each other's incarnations all the time. The energies we
project to each other, the way we think of each other, the feelings we surround
others with, the looks we give, the tones of voice, the words we use: all
these are touches. But are they touches that help us to incarnate and help
the incarnation of another, or do they hinder and obstruct? That is what
only we can determine.*

Everyone is looking for love in their lives. It is a basic need.
What we don't always realize is that in order to find that loving
relationship, we have to be able to give love. And often, being able
to give love depends on being able to love that self from which the
love is given.

I think one of the most difficult tasks for many people is to be
able to love themselves. Are we even capable of receiving love from
another if we can't love ourselves? We will be drawn to the loving
relationship but may be unable to take in the gift which is offered
because we don't feel worthy of it.

As David says, we have an image of what loving is, but there
are many dimensions to love, many shades, and we don't have to
be able to jump straight into full blown affection toward someone
who repels us. We can start simply with perception. Noticing an
existence. I don't have to like this existence, I don't have to invite
this existence into my home, but seeing that it exists? I can do that.
I have the power to choose, and I choose to "see" this other whom I
have trouble feeling love for in any way. It may not seem like much,
but it's a baby step from which further steps can evolve.

For me, seeing means recognizing that this person came here
with the same intent to wholeness that I did. Their life began with
loving intent, and I can hold that perception when I think of them.
Whatever life impacts made them so different from me may not
be something I am capable of seeing right now, but I can see that
there is much that we share: we have a body which gets hot and
cold, experiences hunger and thirst, and into which we had to grow
through infancy and childhood, making mistakes along the way. And

57

we all long for love. From that spring board of 'seeing', with practice and intent, we can find ways to love, and these exercises David has outlined are a great way to begin.

Being loving toward others seems easy for some, but for others it may feel out of reach. I might have to start with seeing myself and acknowledging my own right to exist. Can I love myself? That might feel hard to imagine. But can I just simply see and acknowledge myself? " ...we are each "born" from an act of love within the soul". We can start with that simple truth, recognizing that our just being here began with love. Once we recognize this, it is more likely that we will be able to feel and give love to ourselves and then to others.

It is interesting to note how when we choose to give love, we ourselves are filled with love. There is a warmth, a lightness, which fills us, fills our bodies if we let it, and from there it can be gifted to our world. Starting with loving an object is a good practice, as it rarely is confrontational. We can feel love, acceptance, and honoring of the existence of this object, and as we do that, we can feel love flow toward it from deep within ourselves. Interestingly, eventually we can feel love flowing back from the object to us.

It is when we have practiced loving, loving ourselves and loving that which is other, that we become capable of truly and consciously gifting love to our world. We can enliven and enrich the world around us, being a source of blessing to the lives with whom we share this beautiful Earth.

CHAPTER SIX:
MAKING CONNECTIONS

In Chapter 3, I talked about incarnation as a matter of "bridging a gap", that gap being the differential of life, energy, and consciousness between the soul on its native level or wavelength and the physical world. The result of this is the emergence of an incarnational identity that is an amalgam of qualities and energies of the soul and the world.

But how does this take place?

Let's consider for a moment a person joining a large multi-national corporation as a new employee. There are those—perhaps in the Human Resources department—whose job is to help this person integrate into his or her new position, orienting the new hire to the layout of the office and the building it's in, pointing out the cafeteria for meals, giving whatever personnel instructions are necessary in order to fit in to his or her particular department. At the same time, the new individual is making connections to and learning about the corporation as a whole, its history, its culture, its mission statement, how well it's doing in the marketplace and the role his or her department—and his or her job—plays in the large scheme of things within the company. He or she may be making connections as well with whatever layers of management directly oversee or influence his or her job. And he or she is meeting and making connections with other co-workers who share the same office and perhaps the same work. At the same time, the new employee has a life outside the company and likely responsibilities to others such as family, all of which need to be taken into account as well for his or her job has to fit into the larger context of his or her life.

In other words, a person doesn't just show up one day, walk into an office, sit at a desk, and start work. There are connections to be made, things to be learned in order to provide a smooth transition from being unemployed and outside the company to being employed and integrated into the new job.

A similar process occurs for the soul when it takes incarnation. In a sense, we each become an "employee" of Earth, Inc., working in the Humanity Division. We, too, have to make connections that help us integrate into our new positions.

Many years ago, one of my non-physical colleagues said, "You don't incarnate into a body as much as you incarnate into a system of connections and relationships." At the time, this was a whole new way of looking at things for me. When some years later, I began exploring the incarnational process more deeply, I realized how true this is. It's as if we incarnate into a field of energy woven in the most complex way from a great many strands and threads drawn from the subtle worlds. I called this field our *Incarnational System.*

The Incarnational System

The Incarnational System is a dynamic field make up of the connections and relationships we form on different levels of energy and consciousness in order to engage with the Earth in an embodied way. To illustrate and simplify this field, I divided it into four broad categories of connections. These are:

- The Transpersonal Connections
- The Connections with Nature and the physical world
- The Connections with collective Humanity
- The Personal Connections

If I were to relate these to my earlier example of a person coming to work for a large corporation, then the transpersonal would represent the connections the individual has outside the company, such as with his or her family; Nature and the World would be the corporation as a whole, whereas Humanity would be the department within which the individual is employed. The personal connections would be akin to the specific office, co-workers, and tasks that give particular definition to the individual's daily work experience.

I illustrate these different areas of connection in this way:

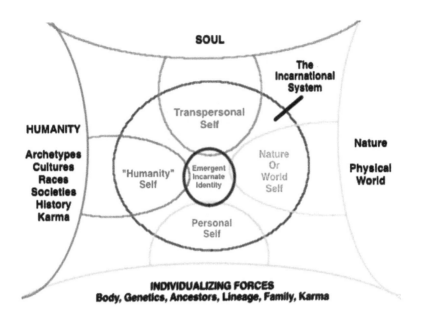

Thus, as the soul enters into the life and energy field of the world, it designates part of itself to make the necessary connections with the forces of nature and the physical world. For convenience, I call this our "Nature" or "World Self"; it has a particular affinity with the land, the natural environment and the wild creatures that make up the Earth.

Similarly there is part of the Soul that has to connect with the collective energy of incarnate Humanity as a whole. A person incarnating in the 21st century is not becoming part of the same humanity that existed in 2000 B.C.E. or in the Seventeenth Century. The incoming soul needs to take account of and connect with the changes that have taken place, connecting with the archetypes, cultures, races, societies, history, and, yes, the collective karma and habits, of the human race as it is at the time of its incarnation. The part of the soul that has this particular affinity and task I call our "Humanity Self".

While part of the soul incarnates, part of it remains in touch with the soul levels and continues to function at a transpersonal level. To accommodate this, a part of the soul which might be called our

"Transpersonal Self" acts as a conduit or link of communication—primarily through the energy of Sovereignty—between the soul-consciousness that incarnates and becomes part of the emerging incarnate identity and the soul-consciousness that remains active in the soul realms.

Finally, there are what I think of as "individualizing forces" that take the broad, universal energy and qualities of soul consciousness and focus it into a specific, particular form using such tools as the physical body, its genetic characteristics, the ancestral line and lineage, the family connections, personal karma or habits, and the like. It is our "Personal Self" that is most in touch with and influenced by these forces.

In effect, there are, broadly speaking, four "selves" that interact to create an emergent incarnate identity, and they do so through the connections of the Incarnational System.

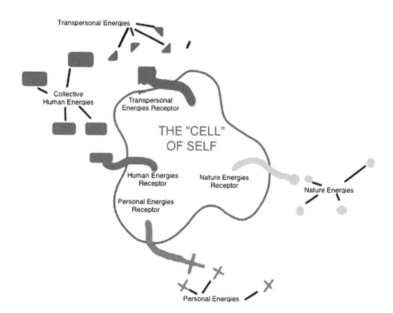

One way I think about this is using the metaphor of a cell. There are places on the cell membrane that act as receptor sites; in effect, they are the sensory organs of the cell, giving it information about what is happening in its environment. At these receptor sites, specialized proteins extend out from the interior of the cell into the surrounding environment. Each such protein is structured in such a way as to match up with a certain complementary molecule in the cell's surroundings. When the receptor protein encounters such a matching molecule, it changes its shape, and this change carries information into the body of the cell itself, triggering a response of some nature.

I can think of each of the four "selves" of the Incarnational System as a kind of "protein" of consciousness and subtle energy. When it encounters a matching energy in the environment, it forms a connection. Thus in the "cell of self", as the picture above shows, there are "receptors" for the transpersonal, natural, human, and personal energies "floating" in the subtle environment of the individual. Each such "receptor" pulls its complementary energy into the life of the individual, weaving it in some manner into the emergence of the incarnate identity.

However, each of these different subtle energies are themselves part of much larger systems. Thus, when the Incarnational System forms a connection with forces and energies from Nature through the mediation of the "Nature Self", the part of the incarnating soul that carries those particular affinities, it is connecting to something much vaster than itself. Simplifying the process, I would say there is a consequent pull out into the larger system as well as a pull into the individuating Incarnational System. It is not a given that all these different subtle energies will automatically blend and weave together to form the Incarnational System and become a harmonious, coherent part of the individual's incarnate identity. There is also the potential that each of the connections can pull away from that individual wholeness, pulling the Incarnational System away from coherence and integration into incoherency and a loss of wholeness. There must be another force at work to hold the various differing energies together in a dynamic and emerging wholeness.

This force is one we have already discussed: the force of Sovereignty. Sovereignty is the organizing, synthesizing, integrating principle at work at the heart of the Incarnational System and its connections, blending them into coherency and wholeness. And underlying and empowering Sovereignty is love.

LOVE & THE INCARNATIONAL SYSTEM

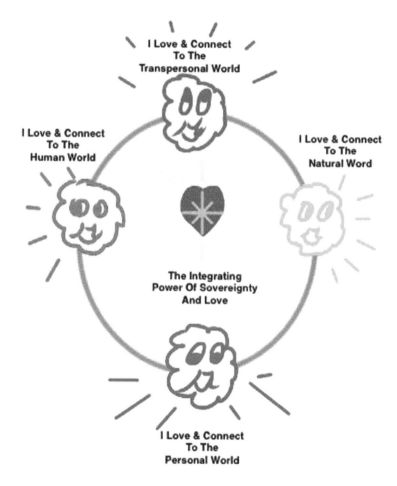

I Love & Connect
To The
Transpersonal World

I Love & Connect
To The
Human World

I Love & Connect
To The
Natural Word

The Integrating
Power Of Sovereignty
And Love

I Love & Connect
To The
Personal World

As we discussed in the last chapter, love is at the core of the incarnational process. It provides the "melting," unitive, alchemical, combining power that draws different elements together into a coherent and integrated wholeness.

The Incarnational System, held together by Sovereignty and Love, provides the necessary connections that weave the soul into the life of the world, but it also serves another purpose. To understand this, we need to look again at the nature of the "gap" between the soul level and the incarnate world.

There are different ways this difference could be described, but I like the image of jugglers.

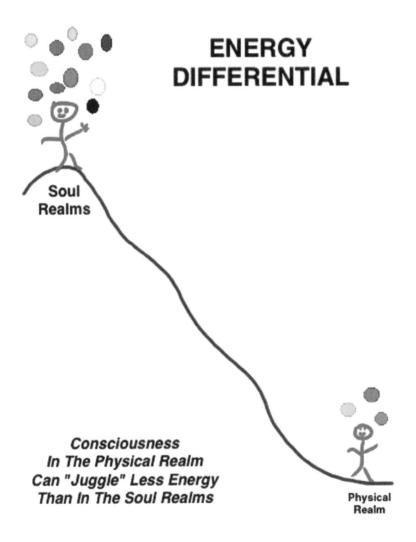

ENERGY DIFFERENTIAL

Soul Realms

Consciousness
In The Physical Realm
Can "Juggle" Less Energy
Than In The Soul Realms

Physical Realm

In the soul realms, the soul is like a juggler juggling twelve balls of energy in the air. In the physical realm, though, incarnate consciousness can only handle three balls at once. The difference between twelve balls and three balls is the energy differential between the soul and the incarnate identity. But when the soul incarnates, what happens to these extra nine balls?

This is where the Incarnational System comes into play. The energy is distributed throughout the whole Incarnational System. In effect, the World, Humanity, and the individualizing forces become allies with the transpersonal forces in helping to bring and hold the energy of the soul into incarnation, acting through the connections and relationships of the Incarnational System.

Think of a four-hundred pound man leaping from a burning building. If a single fireman tried to catch him, he would be flattened and crushed. But a team of firemen holding a net can catch him as the kinetic energy of the falling man will be distributed throughout the whole system. No one fireman has to bear the brunt of all that weight and all that energy.

The Incarnational System is like a net to catch the soul as it descends into matter. It is like a team of jugglers there to catch all the balls so that none of them is dropped and none are lost.

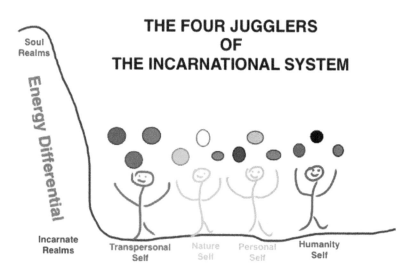

Another metaphor I use to describe the function of the Incarnational System is that of plasma.

Plasma is the fourth state of matter, the other three being solid, liquid, and gas. Plasma is a highly charged and normally super-hot state of matter that is found at the heart of stars. Scientists have known of it for a long time, but they were hampered in their ability to study it as there was no physical material capable to withstanding the intense heat of the plasma. Any container would simply vaporize. However, because plasma is electrically charged, it was discovered that it could be contained in a non-physical magnetic field called a "magnetic bottle." Through the use of such a "bottle," scientists could capture and hold the fire of the sun.

The soul with all its complexity and energy is a kind of "plasma" of consciousness and life. The Incarnational System, through its various connections and relationships, provides the subtle equivalent of a "magnetic bottle" to hold the fire of our living sacredness. It does this by being an alchemical chalice of love. It can draw in and hold the various creative and formative energies from its environment and transform them from being "nature stuff", "world stuff", "humanity stuff", and so on into the substance and energy of the incarnate identity and individuality.

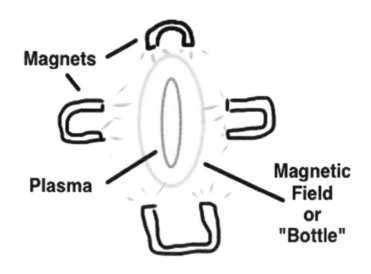

Holding Fire

"Fire" of Soul

"Plasma" of Sacredness

Transpersonal Self

Incarnational System

Humanity or Species Self

World or Nature Self

Personal Self

The Alchemical Chalice Of Love

The idea of the Incarnational System plays an important part in the understanding of Incarnational Spirituality as a whole, but for our purposes here, the key thing lies in realizing that our unique, individual subtle energy field is made up of elements drawn from a variety of other sources, each of which comes with its own identity and its own agendas. The potential exists for dispersal and incoherence. Our Sovereignty and the boundaries it creates are among the forces that work towards our wholeness and integration. But there is another force that is every bit as powerful and important, and this is the power of our love.

As I have said, there is love at the core of our Incarnational System, but this love can be further augmented and empowered by the love we bring to our various "selves" and connections. We have the power to enhance our own wholeness and integration. In effect, our conscious self becomes a partner to the "selves" of the Incarnational System, and in this collaboration and partnership we will find a greater strength than if we are at war with ourselves.

Over the years in doing classes and workshops, I've encountered people who felt shame at being human and were emotionally in conflict with their connection to humanity. Others felt conflicted about their "animal natures", so called, or about their personalities and personal egos. Some were afraid of anything to do with the transpersonal. Yet all of these elements are part of who we are; they form the weave of connections and energies that enable us to be a part of this world. The original message I had that we "incarnate into a system", which eventually led to the insights about the Incarnational System, was itself part of a larger discussion about the need to love ourselves—and all parts of ourselves—if we wish to achieve wholeness. There are natural tensions in the system that can pull apart to follow different agendas. The humanity part of us, for instance, may not wish to listen to the impressions and insights coming from the "Nature Self", desiring instead to pay attention only to a human need to dominate whatever the environmental costs. Or our personal side wishes to follow its own desires and not listen to what the transpersonal side may say. And the reverse can happen, that a person listens so much to his or her transpersonal levels that the personal self is starved and allowed to atrophy.

In other words, the Incarnational System contains a potential for disorder and disintegration, and we can further this through our internal conflicts and privileging one part over another. Yet this very potential gives the Incarnational System a dynamic, creative tension that can enhance our life if we can strengthen its coherency and integration. Our love can do this: love consciously and intentionally given to all the parts of who we are, seeing each "self" as a partner in creating a larger wholeness.

BRINGING LOVE TO THE SYSTEM

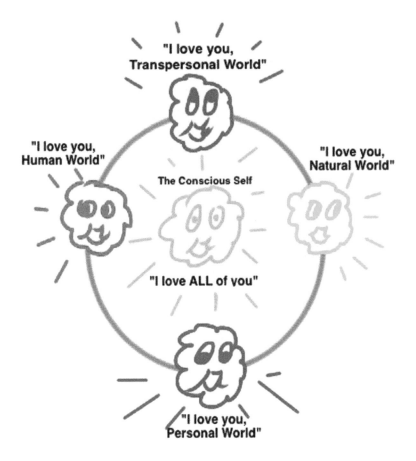

Maybe we can't fully love all the parts of ourselves right away. But this is why we learned about the spectrum of love. At the very least, we can see and acknowledge that a certain part exists, and from there, we can begin to move up the spectrum.

The Incarnational System is our deep connection to the life and energies of the world. It integrates us into the Earth at many levels.

As we stand in the center of this system with a presence of love, we are loving the world as well, and we are empowering the emergence of greater wholeness in our own lives.

EXERCISE FOR CHAPTER SIX

Discovering Presence

This is one of the earliest exercises I developed for Incarnational Spirituality. Its purpose is to create a felt sense of that part of you that draws all your various inner "selves" into a wholeness. Presence is the expression of that state of wholeness, incorporating both personal and transpersonal, worldly and human elements. It is also the presence of your Sovereignty, your inner fire of sacred beingness that can, through love, create and maintain wholeness.

Important note: In part of this exercise, you are asked to attune to your everyday personal self. This is not an exercise in judgment or self-criticism. There may be things you don't like about yourself, are ashamed of, and wish to change or improve. That is perfectly fine, but that perception is not part of this particular exercise. You may certainly make an honest appraisal of yourself; indeed, this is essential. But do not get into self-blame or criticism or begin listing ways in which you can change and do better. That is another kind of work you can engage in at another time.

1. Find yourself a comfortable place to stand. This is a moving exercise, one in which you will be turning to face the four directions. In each direction you will face and attune to an aspect of your Incarnational System, eventually drawing them all into the alchemical Chalice of your incarnation.

2. Imagine yourself in a sacred or magical circle, a protected and honored space—an emergence space--that is dedicated to this exercise.

3. TRANSPERSONAL SELF:
   Choose any direction and face it. In this direction is a vision of your Soul, your Transpersonal Self, the part of you that is connected to the inner worlds and to transcendent states of communion and unity, spirit and creativity. Take a moment to reflect on being part of Spirit, part of a vast ecology of life and consciousness not limited to physical reality. What does

this mean to you? What energy does it carry for you? What do you feel in its presence? What is your felt sense of your transpersonal nature? Be honest in your appraisal.

Take a moment to honor your Soul and Transpersonal Self. Appreciate it, give it thanks for its contribution to the wholeness of who you are. It is a channel through which Sacredness—your sacredness—can flow and act. Embrace it with your love.

4. NATURE (OR WORLD) SELF:
Turn ninety degrees and face a new direction. In this direction is a vision of your Nature Self, your World Self, your Earthiness, the part of you that is connected to the physical world and to nature as a whole. Take a moment to reflect on being part of this world, part of the biosphere, part of the realm of physical matter, part of the Earth. This part of you connects you to the World Soul. It connects you to ecology, to nature, to plants and animals everywhere. It connects you to the land, to seas and mountains, plains and valleys, swamps and deserts. What does this mean to you? What energy does it carry for you? What do you feel in its presence?

Take a moment to honor your Nature self. Appreciate it, give it thanks for its contribution to the wholeness of who you are. It is a channel through which Sacredness—your sacredness—can flow and act. Embrace it with your love.

5. PERSONAL SELF:
Turn ninety degrees and face a new direction. In this direction is a vision of your Everyday, Personal Self. Take a moment to reflect on your uniqueness as a person. Reflect on what defines you, what makes you different from others. This is your ordinary, everyday self. What does this mean to you? What energy does it carry for you? What do you

feel in its presence? What is your felt sense of your personal self? Be honest in your appraisal, but do not engage in self-criticism.

Take a moment to honor your personal, everyday self. Appreciate it, give it thanks for its contribution to the wholeness of who you are. It is a channel through which Sacredness—your sacredness—can flow and act. Embrace it with your love.

6. HUMANITY (OR SPECIES) SELF:
Turn ninety degrees and face a new direction. In this direction is a vision of your Humanness, the part of you that connects you to the human species and to human culture, creativity, and civilization. Take a moment to reflect on being human. Your humanity gives you various attributes and potentials not shared by other creatures on this earth. Your humanness makes you part of a planetary community of other human beings, part of the spiritual idea or archetype of Humanity. What does this mean to you? What energy does it carry for you? What do you feel in its presence? What is your felt sense of your humanness? Be honest in your appraisal, but do not engage in self-criticism. Humanity may have its faults and it may behave badly in the world, but that is not the focus here.

Take a moment to honor your human self. Appreciate it, give it thanks for its contribution to the wholeness of who you are. Being human is a channel through which Sacredness—your sacredness—can flow and act. Embrace it with your love.

7. PRESENCE:
Turn ninety degrees back to the direction you were facing when you started. At this time, turn your attention to yourself at the center of these four "Selves," these four elements of your Incarnational System: your personal self, your human

self, your world self, your transpersonal self. You are the point of synthesis where they all meet, come together, blend, partner, cooperate, merge, and co-create wholeness.

Feel the energies of these four selves, these four directions, flowing into and through you, blending, merging, and creating an open, evocative, creative space within you. Feel what emerges from this space. Feel the holistic Presence of your unique incarnation and sovereignty rising around you and within you, enfolding you, supporting you, becoming you. Feel the Presence that embrace, includes, grows out of and is larger than the four selves you have acknowledged and honored.

Who are you as this incarnational Presence? What is the felt sense of who you are?

At the same time, feel the love that honors and holds these four aspects of you and of the world together, enabling them to collaborate and work in partnership. This love is the fire of Sacredness within you. Honor this and honor yourself for your ability to hold it in your Presence.

8. Stay in the circle feeling the reality and energy of your Presence for as long as feels comfortable to you. When you begin to feel restless, tired, or distracted, just give thanks. Give thanks to your wholeness, to your Presence, and to the Sacredness from which it emerges and which it represents within the ecology of your incarnate life. Absorb, integrate, and ground as much of the felt sense and energy of this Presence as you can or wish into your body, into your mind and feelings, into yourself. Then step forward out of your circle, thus ending this exercise.

Julia's Commentary

If, as was discussed in the last chapter, we can start with 'seeing' ourselves without naming or judging, just perceiving and then acknowledging our own existence and our right to exist, we can begin to touch the love for our incarnate selves which leads to our wholeness. And our wholeness is what allows us to fully engage with the incarnational intent to be a blessing to the planet.

It is good to note which parts of the previous exercise come easiest to you. What parts are you most comfortable with? For some, it might be the transpersonal while for others that might feel out of reach. For some, nature might be easier to connect with while others may be more attuned to the human world. Whichever comes easiest, that sense of attunement to and love for that particular part, can help enliven and bring love into the rest of the parts of the incarnational system. Ultimately, we come to love all of these parts, for they are the whole. We cannot eliminate any one without losing the integrity of our incarnate life. Each of these 'selves' is an invaluable piece of the art form that is you.

When we are able to stand in the center of this system of selves, we hold all of the parts. Then we find we are able to love each of those parts, even the ones which we feel challenged by. All of these parts are like sentient beings, and they all pull in different directions. The physical part may be driven by survival needs like hunger, or comfort, or sexual drives. These may pull in a direction which conflicts with my emotional parts which might seek security or love or safety. I may value being nonjudgmental and yet feel critical of things around me which upsets the harmony I seek. We are pulled in different directions which activate different parts of ourselves, but it is important in the midst of all this to recognize that we also are a wholeness. We can acknowledge the different voices within us and look for the way each one contributes to make us uniquely ourselves unlike any other incarnate being, including the parts we don't like. We can learn to love those parts that may be giving us trouble by understanding the gifts they offer and choosing to redirect our response to the challenges they bring.

We have the capacity to choose our focus. For example, if I have a natural tendency to be critical, one gift of that is the ability to spot flaws, which is very necessary for precision. But there are situations in which it may not be my responsibility to be precise. That is when I choose to step back and allow another person to take charge in their own way. I can acknowledge to myself my great critical eye when I see that picture askew on my neighbor's wall, but then I can ask that part to relax and appreciate or ignore the tilt. Yes, it takes practice. We have within us the capacity to hold and consciously nurture the integrity of the system, and as we do so, something emerges which is our Presence; the Presence that is also holding it all together, holding the parts in relationship and, when we are conscious or intentional about it, in a blending of communion and enhancement.

Your Presence expresses the uniqueness of the art form that is you; it is part of your gift to the diversity, the richness, and the wholeness of humanity and of the earth. There is no other voice that is like yours to add to the song of the universe.

CHAPTER SEVEN:
THE MEDIATED IDENTITY

In the previous chapter, we saw that the entry of the soul into incarnation is made possible by a web of energetic connections and relationships with the earth and with humanity. I called this web our Incarnational System. It's an important factor in enabling the soul to blend its energy with that of the incarnate world.

However, there are additional elements at work that act as mediating influences in assisting the soul in manifesting in the physical world. In fact, one of the key characteristics of incarnation is that we have a *mediated identity*.

Let me explain what I mean.

As I type this, I look down at my hands on the keyboard and I think, *These are my hands. My fingers are typing on the keys.* And they *are* my hands. They are expressing the thoughts that I, David Spangler, am having as I write these words.

At the same time, they are also collections of individual cells divide up into muscle, bone, sinew, skin, joints, blood vessels, blood cells, and so on. In order for me to write these words, millions of individual lives are at work enabling my thoughts to be transmitted to my hands, my fingers to dance about the keys, and so forth.

As I write, I notice that one of my fingers isn't working as well as it used to. One of its joints has become stiff and at times painful. My will to write is as strong as ever, but this finger's ability to join with its brethren in hitting the right keys with grace and ease is not what it was. No matter how much I think "Be Supple" at this finger and its joint, it persists in its stiffness. Obviously, the cells in this part of my finger are not wholly under my control.

And the same is true with other parts of my body which, after seventy years of serving me and expressing my identity, are beginning to exhibit signs of not functioning as well or as fully as I would wish or as I've come to expect.

The fact is that my identity as a soul and as a personality expresses itself through the actions of well over two trillion body cells and associated microbes that live in and on my body. My identity

79

is mediated by the cooperative effort of over two trillion lives and identities other than my own. Most of the time, these lives cooperate and match my identity and its characteristics and wishes very well. But sometimes, they don't, and my body does things or develops problems which it would not if it configured perfectly to my soul and my consciousness. At the very least, as my body ages, it looks less like how I feel inside. I look in the mirror and I do not see the self I experience myself as being.

Of course, in this perspective, I'm seeing my identity—and yours—as something non-physical and spiritual in essence, not as a product of my physical DNA. My DNA is part of the individualizing genetic lineage that forms part of the "personal" or "body" node in the Incarnational System, as we saw in a previous chapter. Our identities are soul-based, not body-based, but they are certainly anchored in and expressed through our bodies. And our bodies are communities of lives organized as cells, tissues, organs, and so on. From the standpoint of Incarnational Spirituality, these cellular and microbial lives have their own spiritual identities, their own unique life force, their own connection to the Sacred. A liver cell in my body is performing a needed function that maintains my presence on earth, but it's also a being in its own right with its own kind and level of consciousness, life and spiritual evolution.

Although this principle of mediation is most clearly seen on the physical level in the form of the cells that make up our bodies, it holds true in the subtle side of our lives as well. Our subtle bodies (or "sheaths" as they are sometimes called) are made up of patterns generated by the soul but also of energy patterns taken up from the world through the connections made in the Incarnational System. These patterns form energy structures within us—metaphorically like "energy cells"—that can in turn create ways of thinking and feeling that arise seemingly automatically within the individual, though they can be changed by conscious awareness and intent.

Here's an example. When a soul takes incarnation, one connection it forms is with the particular subtle energy of the location on Earth where it will be born. It connects to the land where its parents are living. How strong a connection this is depends on other variables, but I believe it's there to some degree in all incarnations. This means that part of the energy that is absorbed and used to fashion the personal subtle field is taken from the unique energy of a particular physical environment. This becomes part of the individual's subtle body, a kind of "cell" if you wish, through which the incarnate identity will manifest.

I was born in the United States in the State of Ohio, but my parents and I moved to California when I was four years old. I didn't go back to the State of my birth until thirty years later. My parents had moved back to Ohio, and I went there to visit them. Consciously, I felt no ties at all to the State, so it was a total surprise when, as the plane I was on was landing at the Dayton airport, I felt a surge of energy rising up from the land greeting me and I felt a corresponding response from within me. Something deep within the structure of my subtle energy body responded to the energy of the land. I felt like I was coming to a familiar place, though I have almost no memories of the four years I lived in Ohio.

This response had nothing to do with the State, which is a human political construct, but it was connected to the energy of the land itself. I realized that something in me shared the energy of this land and reached out to the world through it. I didn't feel any desire to move back to Ohio, but I felt like part of me had been re-energized and empowered by contact with a familiar vibration.

This got me to thinking about the power the presence of a "land energy" may have within a person's personal energy field. For some people, it's not a strong influence and can be overridden by other influences or by conscious thought. For instance, in my own case, though I felt—and continue to feel when I attune to it—the presence of the Ohio land vibration in my personal field, it didn't lead me to move back to that land from my home in Washington State. On the other hand, someone else may feel such a connection to the land of her birth that she can't imagine being anywhere else. How many wars that are fought over land may have their origin—or at least a contributing influence—from a land vibration incorporated into the subtle fields of the people involved in the conflict?

The point is that the soul channels its identity through subtle fields that in part are made up of energies generated by the soul and reflecting its characteristics and in part made up of energies drawn from the various collective fields that make up the environment in which the soul is incarnating. Such energies may come from natural sources, like the land itself, or from human sources, such as the collective energy of a town or a nation, a race or a culture, a religion or a philosophy. They form a "field of influence" which can serve a purpose in helping the soul connect to the collectives they represent but which can also create motivations and pressures that cause the individual to act in ways that represent the interests of the collective but not necessarily the intents of his or her own soul.

For that matter, we can see this same dynamic reflected on a more conscious, everyday level. We all pick up and take on ideas, attitudes, opinions, feelings, beliefs, and so on from others—from parents, teachers, religious figures, political figures, artists and performers, and so on—that do not come from our own original thinking or from our own depths but which we use to navigate our world. For instance, my father, if he could help it, never used anything but Shell gasoline in his car. Years later, long after I'd started to drive, I realized one day that I was doing the same thing. Looking to fill up, I would automatically look for a Shell station even if another brand of gas might be selling for less at another station. I had taken on a mental habit from my father and it had become like a "cell" in my mental energy field.

Of course, we all need to learn things from our environment and do so as we grow up. I'm thinking here of those elements in our psyche that we simply absorb without thought and then use to express ourselves. They form a psychic structure that shapes how we engage the world. Like our physical cells, it "mediates" us to the world around us in automatic ways. Fortunately, it's a structure we can change anytime by thinking through it into new ways of being and choosing new ways of thinking and acting.

Incarnation is not simply the entry of a soul into a body. It is the collaboration of the soul with a variety of forces and beings that together mediate the soul's presence into a "paper towel" universe made up of infinite particles and individualities. The coming together in cooperation of many of these individualities operating at various levels of consciousness allows for a greater, more complex individuality and consciousness to manifest.

Thus we have a picture of the soul as it moves into incarnation entering into progressive fields and degrees of collaboration and cooperation, from the Incarnational System through the field of subtle influences created by the subtle energies the soul takes on to the physical body itself with its community of trillions of cells. As one of my non-physical colleagues once said, "Incarnation is the art of living as a mediated identity."

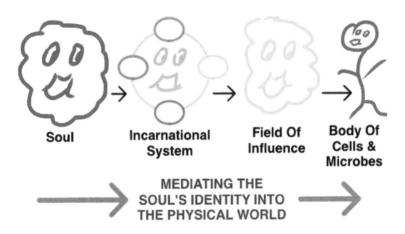

| Soul | Incarnational System | Field Of Influence | Body Of Cells & Microbes |

MEDIATING THE SOUL'S IDENTITY INTO THE PHYSICAL WORLD

EXERCISES FOR CHAPTER SEVEN

Honoring And Blessing The Cells

1. Stand in your Sovereignty and Presence
2. Project your consciousness via your imagination into any tissue in your body. Take a moment to bless this tissue and the body of which it is a part.
3. Attuned to this tissue, project your consciousness and presence into a cell within this tissue. Take a moment to bless this cell and all others like it.
4. Within the cell, project your consciousness out to all the cells of your body, honoring and blessing them for their individuality, their service, their participation in making your life possible.
5. Now imagine all the living cells—the microbes and bacteria—that live on or in your body in community with your body's cells and which serve the wholeness and well-being of your body. Honor and bless all these microbial lives that make up the community of your body and serve to mediate your soul's identity into the world.
6. Bring your consciousness back into your full self. Stand in your Sovereignty and Presence.
7. What, if anything, did you bring back from this attunement to your body and its service of mediation?

Reflection

Take some time to think about "psychic structures"—ideas, beliefs, habits, feelings—that you may have simply taken up from the environment and may use in expressing yourself without really having thought about them.

In other words, reflect on just what in your life may be "mediating" you.

Julia's Commentary

Incarnation is the art of living as a mediated identity.

It is hard to really imagine and encompass the complexity of the process of incarnation, not to mention the millions of influences involved. Cells, bacteria, microscopic particles impacting our bodies—people with allergies are very aware of some of these. It can seem overwhelming to try to imagine having a conscious relationship with them all. Add to that the influences of subtle interactions with humans, cultures, languages, and then just the many voices in our own bodies and minds. How do we integrate all this into a conscious wholeness?

Simply imagining all the myriad lives that serve our incarnation and feeling gratitude for their assistance is a good start. It makes loving ourselves a whole other concept. This is not a self-indulgent concept of ego-aggrandizement. It is actually an appreciation of the whole magnificence and mystery of the incarnational field and all the lives and relationships which make it happen.

This exercise is predominantly about becoming conscious of the rich influences surrounding us in our incarnate life. How do they influence us? How do they connect me with my world, my culture, my family? How do they confine and constrict or support and enhance my interactions with those in my world? What supports my deepest intent and what doesn't serve me? When I recognize something which doesn't serve my highest purpose, how do I reset my involvement with it?

There are many healing and therapeutic approaches to help us address the countless disparate elements within us. They enable us to be aware of the ideas, feelings and patterns that we take up which we then use to express ourselves. Are they really expressing who we are? By seeing them, listening to the voices and parts they represent and learning of the gifts they offer and the challenges they also offer, we stand more clearly in the Presence which helps that incarnational fire burn more brightly and more clearly.

CHAPTER EIGHT:
HOLDING

In the previous chapters, we've looked at incarnation as a system and as a "mediated" activity. In so doing, we've been looking at how our incarnation is made up of—and made possible by—different interacting parts. We can experience this for ourselves. How often do we feel that there are a variety of "selves" living inside us? There's the self we take to work, the self that appears when dealing with our family, the self we wear when we're having fun, our private self, and so on. There are various philosophies and methodologies of psychology and therapy that focus on this idea of multiple inner selves. In extreme pathological conditions, the individual may disassociate and fragment into several different personalities, which may or may not be aware of the others.

At the same time that we can identify different aspects or parts of ourselves, we also experience ourselves as a single person. Our bodies with their trillions of cells may be akin to a hive, but we don't feel like a hive. Or to use a different metaphor, while there may be many working parts "under the hood", we feel like we're driving a whole car, not a collection of components.

Something binds all of our "moving" parts together in wholeness so that we experience ourselves as a singularity, not a multiplicity. This "something" I call the Principle of Holding.

We're all familiar with holding. We hold things all day long. A moment ago I was holding a tea cup which in turn was holding my tea for me to drink as I sit here writing. But there's more to holding than just this. What I call the Principle of Holding is a creative act. Specifically, *Holding is the act of creating a space in which a unique activity can take place.* It is this "space" which is important. For instance, what holds the tea in my tea cup is the space that the sides of the cup create. The substance of the cup itself doesn't intermingle with the liquid molecules of the tea (at least I hope not!); one atom of porcelain is not attached to and holding one atom of tea. But the atoms of porcelain shaped in a particular way form a space that can be filled with the tea.

Holding tea, though, is a passive act. The Principle of Holding is very active. So let's think of another example. Let's think of the rules of Poker. These rules hold the unique activity of Poker. Within these rules, one isn't playing Blackjack, Old Maid, or some other card game. One is not reading about Poker, either, or using Poker hands in an oracular way to divine the future (though they are being used, one hopes, to gain one's fortune!). When playing Poker, one's activity is constrained and contained by the agreed-upon rules of the game, but within these boundaries, within the unique "space" created by these rules, a dynamic and ever-changing activity can take place in which there will be winners and losers and money will change hands.

The tea cup holds my tea. The rules of Poker hold the game of Poker. Likewise the rules of Baseball hold that game. Also, the walls of my house hold the unique space in which my home comes into being.

Let me repeat: *Holding is an activity that creates a space within which a unique activity or set of activities may unfold.* It creates this space by forming and maintaining boundaries. The rules of Poker are boundaries that determine what can and cannot be done with the cards and what the cards mean. The sides of the tea cup forms the ovoid space into which tea can be poured. And the intent and love of the soul creates the boundaries that hold the space within which our incarnation develops and unfolds.

Here we can see in a different way the function of the Incarnational System and the mediating forces and identities—such as the identities of my body's cells. The Incarnational System of connections and relationships—simplified for our purposes into four major categories—could be said to form the bowl of an incarnational chalice, while the mediating forces that make up the subtle energy fields and the physical body form the stem and base that connect to the Earth. Together they form a space in which the living fire of the soul's presence—the "plasma" of the Soul—can be held, giving life and energy to nourish the unfoldment of the incarnate life.

88

THE INCARNATIONAL CHALICE
(Holding The Sacred Fire)

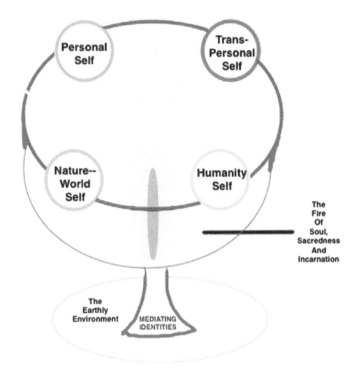

Holding is a universal principle active at all levels of existence. The Sacred holds the universe in its love, creating the conditions—the space of beingness and potential—that allow the cosmos to exist, flourish, and develop. Gaia, the World Soul, forms the boundaries and holds the space that allows planetary life to evolve. The Soul creates and holds a space that allows a physical incarnation to exist and hopefully develop and flourish as well.

The important realization for us is that Holding is something we can do. It's not just for Gods or Souls or Planetary Beings. We can hold ourselves and the world around us in our love, deliberately creating a space for blessing and unfoldment.

When we bring love into our acts of Holding, we create a special space indeed. When a child is in distress and a mother sits and forms a lap, she is creating a space in which she can hold and comfort the child. As a loving space, it can help the child find peace again. When we hold a loved one, we are creating a space in which mutuality and a loving relationship can emerge. Love creates spaces that nourish and empower. It is exactly such a space that the soul creates through its love that allows our incarnation to unfold.

We are all "space-creators". We fill our lives with "chalices of Holding". There are three main ones that form part of our daily lives, even though we may not realize we are creating and holding them.

The first is the chalice of our personality in which our transpersonal and personal sides, the spiritual and the physical, are brought together to form an integrated, unique, generative wholeness.

The second is the chalice of our connections and relationships in which we join with others to invoke and hold what we could not manifest by ourselves: the greater spirit of our humanity.

The third is the chalice of the earth in which we blend with the natural world to allow new patterns to emerge that bless all life on the earth, not just our own.

The capacity to create inner "chalices," loving "spaces" or conditions of heart and mind that can hold energy and spirit, hold each other and ourselves, hold the earth, and hold sacredness is an integral part of the incarnational process and a skill that we can learn and apply.

Obviously, we do not always hold ourselves well, or others either. We can create evil spaces of violence, abuse, and bondage; we create spaces for activities that damage ourselves and others and generate suffering. It is the tragedy of humanity. But the fact that we can use this principle for harm does not negate that it can be used for healing and for empowerment. There is a whole art of blessing that is based in the Principle of Holding, for what is blessing but a particular kind of space that enhances the flow and expression of sacredness within whatever is held in that space?

Incarnation is an act of Holding. The soul holds its Incarnational System, drawing all the various connections and linkages into coherency, integrating them with its Sovereignty. The soul holds its body with all its living cells. The soul holds all the mediating forces that enable it to express its identity in the incarnate realms. And it does so through love.

EXERCISES FOR CHAPTER EIGHT

The Lap

This exercise is very simple: sitting down and forming a lap. A lap is a physical form of holding. When we sit, our bodies form a kind of bowl or cup. Imagine kids climbing into a lap: it is a place of love, comfort, healing, and transformation. Imagine when you climbed into a lap and how good and safe it felt.

In this exercise, simply sit down and form a lap. Go through the following elements as you do so, exploring the felt sense of each. Inherent in the lap is your power of holding.

Physical:

The physical action of this exercise is simplicity itself. From a standing position, you simply sit down, allowing your legs to form a lap. Be aware of the physical sensation and felt sense of being a lap. Feel the relaxation of sitting but at the same time the power and receptivity of forming a lap. Explore the felt sense of the space that is created in front of you, around you, and within you when you sit and form a lap.

Emotional:

Feel the power of being a space of holding. In your lap, you are forming a space of comfort, a space of healing, a space of encouragement and upliftment. In this space, negativity can be received and transformed as you hold a presence of peace, of love, and of strength.

Mental:

Your mind is also a lap. It is a cup that holds your thoughts. As you sit, let your mind go beyond the contents of any thoughts you may be holding. Let it simply appreciate the power of holding thoughts. Appreciate your mental space, the spaciousness of your mind. If thoughts come within this space, simply welcome them and let them sit in your mind-lap for a time, then move on. Remember, you are holding them, they are not holding you. You create and own the space they occupy. Sit in that space, be at peace, and feel the power of your mind to be a lap.

"Magical"/Energetic:

The cup is the oldest of magical images. It is the grail of the sacred, the cauldron of magic and wisdom, the cooking pot that creates nourishment, the womb of life, the cup that holds the cosmos. Your lap is this space, this grail, this cauldron, this womb, and this cup. When you sit and a lap is formed, you are in resonance with this primal container and its spaciousness—the womb of God from which new life is born.

Spiritual:

Sitting, your lap is the presence of the sacred. It is a place of love, a place to receive and comfort pain and suffering, a place of healing, a place of rebirth and regeneration. In the space of your lap you are in resonance with the sacred space that holds all things and allows them to be. God is a lap!

In doing this exercise, simply sit and as you do so, work through these levels of sensation, feeling, thought, energy, and spirit, appreciating the power, the freedom, the sovereignty, and the presence emerging from the simple act of forming a lap.

Self-Lap

This exercise is a variant expression of the Lap exercise focused on yourself.

- Step One: Do the Standing Exercise, feeling your own sovereignty and the power of your individuality.
- Step Two: Draw that power into yourself and do the Lap Exercise, creating a lap both physically and inwardly as a state of mind and being. Let yourself enter a condition of holding empowered by your sovereignty and individuality.
- Step Three: Place yourself in your "lap." Hold yourself. Gather all the parts of you that you can think of, including those parts that you may not like so much or feel cause you problems. You are not doing anything to these parts or selves; you are just holding.

In so doing, gain a felt sense of the Sovereignty and inner presence of will that holds you together in wholeness.. There is in each of us that which is willing to be incarnate, willing to have parts, willing to have a personality, willing to have a body, willing to create a space that holds all the elements of our lives. How do you experience that? What is the felt sense of it to you? What is the love that holds you?

Just let yourself be held and honored by yourself, by your own inner lap.

When you feel this is complete, just stand up and let your lap dissolve. But remember that you continue to hold yourself. As you go through your day, encountering things in your environment that would snag and pull you apart or things in yourself that would divide you and pull you apart, remember the will that holds. Remember your lap. Remember to hold yourself again in love.

You can do this exercise anywhere, anytime that you're sitting down. (Or you can do it in your imagination if you're standing.)

The Holding Touch

This is also a variant of the holding (Lap) exercise given above.

Sit and form a lap. Feel the open space and power of your holding. Feel the love, the acceptance, and the blessing that exists in this holding space before and around you. Imagine the felt sense of this holding space forming a bubble of energy and light that rests in your lap.

Once you have the felt sense of this bubble of holding space firmly in your mind and body, then imagine this bubble flowing into you and moving down both your arms and splitting into ten smaller "bubbles," each moving into the tip of each finger. Imagine that each finger is like a miniature lap carrying the energy and presence of holding.

Now get up and move about your room. Touch things. Take a moment with each thing you touch to feel it being held by the loving, holding power at your fingertips. Visualize that each touch surrounds that which you are touching with a bubble of blessing, love, and appreciation. Pay attention to the felt sense of this at your fingertips, as well as within your body as a whole. Each "fingercup," each "fingerlap," is empowered by the incarnational power of holding. Each finger's touch awakens the possibility of blessing and spaciousness. Each touch honors and empowers the Sovereignty and spirit of that which you touch.

Once you have in mind the felt sense of this, you can manifest this touch of holding anytime, with anyone or anything, during the day. A simple handshake can become a moment of blessing. Remember that energy is NOT flowing from your hands into another. Instead, your fingers create a space of holding for the other within which their own life, their own Soul, their own beingness and light, can generate a blessing. Nor is energy flowing back into you from whatever or whomever you are touching. Your fingers are helping them to become a cup to hold their own blessings of their own beings, not being a cup to receive and hold their energies.

If you feel energy flowing back into you, just see it being held at your fingertips and offered back. This is not an exercise in giving and receiving energy but of holding and creating a space for blessing to emerge however it wishes. If at any time this activity of holding feels tiresome or uncomfortable, just feel the power of holding moving back up your hand and arms away from your fingers, and back into the core of your being, into the light within you. It will be held there until you wish to extend it again.

Julia's Commentary

"What I call the Principle of Holding is a creative act. Specifically, Holding is the act of creating a space in which a unique activity can take place. It is this "space" which is important."

We hold each other in so many ways. It is a very natural part of life which we do unconsciously. Holding is not inherently benign. It is in itself neutral. When we love another, we are holding them. When we hate someone, we are also holding them. The former is a gift of blessing, the later is not. But both are "creating a space within which a unique activity is taking place". How and what we hold will determine the nature of that space. ISIL, for example, is holding space for the re-emergence of the Caliphate. Is this a gift to the people in the Middle East? Many of them do not think so. So it is important to be aware of what we are holding in our lives and how we are doing it. We are powerful beings, and what we do, feel and think impacts our lives and our worlds for good or for bad. But if we are conscious and intentional, and we hold with love, our holding will be for the good and becomes a gift and a blessing.

What is the practice of Holding? Mainly it is the loving intention to support the emergence of the wholeness of whatever is your focus. This loving intention can have many aspects. A boss who is Holding is allowing her employees to become more involved and more creative in their jobs by creating an atmosphere which is caring and supportive of them. She affirms their value and cares for their wellbeing and in so doing encourages them to be their best selves at work. A wonderful example of holding is the coach of the champion Seahawks football team, Pete Carroll. Coach Carroll holds his players in their wholeness and works to find and support the natural talents of the individual players rather than trying to shape the player into what he needs. His coaching style has been described this way by Kristen Gill in an article on what business leaders might learn from the Seahawks coach: *...the relentless competitiveness, the constant quest to identify and maximize the uniqueness of every player and coach, the commitment to a nurturing environment that allows people to be themselves while still being* accountable to the team...in his words, "It's a way that you can help people find heights that they might not have found otherwise... not giving up on them and never failing to be there for them." This is one man's way of practicing holding, though he likely would not call it this.

A therapist can hold mentally through his understanding. He is able to be supportive and detached while holding his client with a loving intent for healing and empowerment. He is not trying to make something specific happen for his clients through mental or emotional manipulation. He is seeing them in wholeness and supporting them in finding their way back to that wholeness through compassionate support and knowledge of healing practices. This is Holding on a mental level.

What would holding look like on an emotional level? Parents hold their children in loving support of their unfoldment into productive adults. They cannot predetermine who these adults will be, so they hold the potential they see. Through their loving empathy, compassion, and understanding, they provide a secure lap for the child to work out his stresses and growth challenges. They understand the needs of the child at her stage of development, and are able to support her as she changes. Parents can't fix the child's problems for them, but they can help them find equilibrium in themselves through love and understanding support. They hold the space for the child to discover the best of who they are.

We have the capacity to intentionally create heart-filled spaces in which we can bless all we come in contact with. We can notice what we hold in our lives, and intentionally choose to invite love into this holding space. When one is practiced, the holding becomes second nature. As David said, "Once you have in mind the felt sense of this, you can manifest this touch of holding anytime, with anyone or anything, during the day." Then each place you go, each person you meet, is blessed and reminded of its sacredness.

CHAPTER NINE:
GRAIL SPACE

Grail Space is an expression of the art of Holding extended energetically into your local environment.

A basic premise of Incarnational Spirituality, as it is of many other spiritual cosmologies, is that everything is ultimately part of a universal Life Force. We all draw from the same well of life. In keeping with the idea of the "paper towel universe", though, this Life Force manifests in infinite individual and collective ways. Thus, atoms are alive, galaxies are alive, and everything in between—stars, planets, human beings, dogs, cats, trees, rose bushes, ants, spiders, bacteria, and so on—is alive as well.

Of course, not everything manifests the universal Life Force in the same way. The living, sentient subtle energy that makes up my couch or my computer desk is not expressing through a biological organism. I can express life and consciousness very differently and with many more options than can the lamp next to my desk.

In a materialistic culture, we don't see objects as being alive. We make a distinction between the organic and the inorganic, and there are significant, important distinctions and differences between them, especially in the physical world. But once we extend our perception and awareness into the realms of subtle energies, then some of these distinctions begin to blur. We can begin to see that everything around us holds this energy of life flowing from the Life Force of the Sacred.

Further, this living energy possesses sentiency, though not necessarily consciousness in the way that we do. What this means is that everything around us is aware of its subtle energy environment to some degree and can respond to it, if only in simple, basic ways. If I love an object, like my coffee cup, the life force within it can sense this, not as an emotion but as a wavelength of energy, and it can respond in kind to some degree.

Most of the time, particularly in a culture which doesn't admit to life within the inorganic world, we go about our daily business unaware of the living energies around us. That we actually live and move in a sea of consciousness and life is usually beyond our perception and thus beyond our understanding or acceptance. Yet, it is true. We are immersed in life and awareness in a multitude of ways, and if we begin to pay attention to it, the Life Force within the world around us can begin to show itself and impress itself upon our consciousness.

The normal condition between a person and an object in our culture is one of energetic non-interaction. We use our objects to accomplish the tasks for which they were designed, but we don't usually think of them as potential allies or collaborators in a universe of subtle energies. They are dead to us, and correspondingly, we are dead to them. Like the proverbial ships passing in the night at sea, our different energy fields touch but do not really engage. What flows between us is minimal and most likely wholly unconscious.

I represent this condition in the following picture:

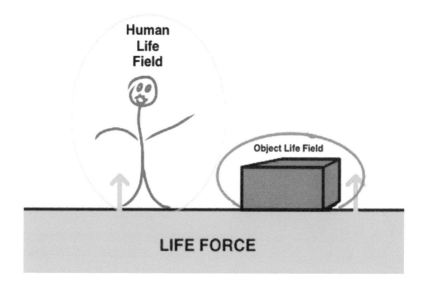

Here we see a human and an object in his or her environment. Both are drawing on the universal life force that permeates all things great and small. Both are radiating their resultant particular field of living energies, but there is little merging or interaction between them.

Through attention, love, habitual use, or some other reason, a person's energy field—his or her "human field"—can expand to embrace an object. This happens naturally; it doesn't have to be a conscious intention *per se*. For instance, when I sit here at my computer and use the keyboard every day, my energy field and that of the computer come into a repeated and sustained contact. My human field interacts with the field of the keyboard and the computer.

When this happens, the energy field of the object in question can begin to vibrate in harmony with the human energy field and take on some of its energy. This can help to shape and enhance the energy field of the object. Just as humans alter the consciousness of animals when we domesticate and live with them, so we "domesticate" the sentiency within objects when we relate to them and engage with them in a regular way. For example, an object that is consistently loved gains within its energetic substance a greater capacity to respond to, hold, and circulate the energy of love within its environment.

This kind of interaction is happening all the time, especially when we love and appreciate an object over time. The same thing happens to us as we are held in the energy fields of vaster subtle beings which can quicken and heighten our own life and consciousness, often in ways of which we are not immediately consciously aware.

However, I can enhance and intensify this process through an act of Holding in which I recognize the life within the things around me and invite this life to collaborate with me in creating a special shared space. It's this energetic condition I call *Grail Space*.

Grail Space is created by invitation, hospitality and collaboration, all of which allow something to emerge that would not have been present otherwise. The Grail Space process acknowledges the life force within all things and seeks to partner with it. This partnering is a form of alliance in that no partner is considered superior to any other. Each is a source of life force and each contributes to the emergence of a larger whole which, like a Grail, can hold an empowering, enriching, and sacred presence within the local environment.

In Grail Space, you reach into the flow of the life force within yourself, perhaps by attuning to your Sovereignty and Self-Light, and then extend that life force to the things around you. In so doing, you are inviting their life force to arise and respond to yours. You are offering yourself to the things around you and inviting them in a hospitable and loving way to do the same to you. You are inviting them to join you in being a large "lap", a field of Holding that can draw forth in greater measure the Life Force of the Sacred for all to share. As they respond and their life force connects with yours, the Grail Space comes into being between you.

In this way, Grail Space is a relational "artifact". It is born of collaboration. One being is not doing something to any other, but all are sharing life as partners to allow a greater presence of life to emerge. In a way, Grail Space as a process reflects Christ's statement that where two or more are gathered in His name, there He is also. In this case, two or more are gathering in the name of Life—the sacred life force within all things—and as a result, a greater Life—a sacred presence of Life—emerges.

GRAIL SPACE
When Life Forces Meet And Blend

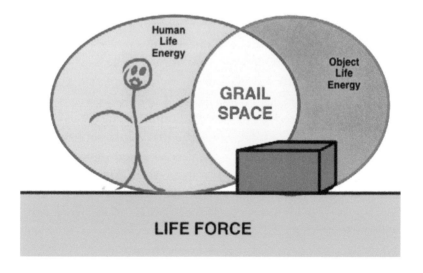

Creating Grail Space is not the same as giving a blessing. In a Grail Space, nothing is being done to anything or on behalf of anything. There is no focus or "target" for the practice. Rather, it is like a collaborative circle of life creating a space together in which a presence may emerge that in turn blesses all the participants.

As a spiritual practice of "horizontal spirituality" and attunement and partnership with the world around me, I create and hold a Grail Space in my home at least once a day. If I'm out somewhere else and it seems appropriate, I will create a Grail Space there as well. It's a silent practice that can be done unobtrusively and in ways that do not impose anything upon a particular environment. If the energy within an environment doesn't seem able to respond—or doesn't wish to—then nothing will happen, and I simply let it go.

Once I was sitting in a doctor's reception room waiting for my appointment. I thought this was a good opportunity to practice Grail Space within that room, so I centered myself in my Sovereignty and Self-Light and acknowledged the presence of life and awareness in the objects in the room around me. I extended my love and living energy field to them and invited them to do the same in return. I felt an immediate sense of response. However, much to my surprise, a small being about two feet high appeared before me to my clairvoyant awareness. It seemed to be a kind of "office spirit" or a being attached in some way to the building. It was something I hadn't experienced before.

"What are you doing?" it asked in both a curious and a challenging tone. I explained about Grail Space and what I was trying to do.

"Human beings don't do that kind of thing!" It spoke in an astonished way as if the natural order of things had somehow come unstuck. "Humans just ignore us."

"Well, this human doesn't ignore you. And yes, I am doing exactly this kind of thing, if you don't mind."

At this point, realizing that I meant what I said and that I really was loving and connecting with the subtle life energies in the room, the being brightened—quite literally, as it became energetically brighter. "That's wonderful!" he said. "Thank you! Please carry on." And with that, it disappeared.

I haven't had an experience like that again, but I regularly feel the lightness that can come into a room when I invite it to hold Grail Space with me. It's a powerful practice that for me is an essential and central part of Incarnational Spirituality.

EXERCISE FOR CHAPTER NINE

Grail Space

When I combine a felt sense of the life in everything around me with a loving appreciation and connection with that life, I have the tools to create a condition of energy and spirit that I call Grail Space after the legendary Holy Grail that held the sacred and transformative blood of Christ. Grail Space is a special act of collaborative holding, one that transforms a sense of space into a felt sense of spaciousness, an acknowledgement and celebration of the sacred presence that is the life within and uniting all things.

Grail Space is a form of blessing but one that is based on partnership and mutual reciprocity rather than on someone doing something to or for another. When I create Grail Space in the room around me, I'm not so much energizing the room as I am engaging with it to jointly manifest a condition in which we are all heightened, deepened and enhanced in our capacity to hold and manifest our innate sacredness. It's not one flame using its light to brighten another. It's many flames joining to form a larger flame that enhances them all.

The Exercise:
- Begin by standing in your own Sovereignty, in the felt sense of your unique identity and your connection to your soul and to the sacred. You can imagine this Sovereignty as a "spine" of Light within you. Use the Standing Exercise if this will help you accomplish this.
- Imagine a universal presence of Life flowing along this spine of Light connecting you to the cosmos above and the earth below. Feel Life ascending and descending and blending in your heart with the unique presence of your own Identity.
- Take a moment to survey your immediate environment, taking note of all the things that are in it. Do so as a witness in a non-judgmental way. Everything in your immediate environment is an expression of this universal Life. Everything you see has its own "spine" of Light and identity, its own flow of

life force.

- Extend your love outward to all these objects around you. As you do, feel the life force within you flow out from your heart and spine into the space around you, inviting the life force in the things around you to flow out to meet your life and connect with you. In this connection, a collaborative communion is formed in which no single source of Light illumines all the others like a sun does its planets but rather all these sources of Light combine together in loving communion and acknowledgement. This shared communion is the Grail Space. What is its felt sense?

- While in this Space, feel how it opens depths within you and within everything around you, becoming a portal of spaciousness and blessing for the world around you, becoming a Grail for a collective sacredness.

- Stay in this Grail Space as long as feels comfortable. When you feel tired or restless, simply draw your life force and attention back into yourself, giving thanks to your energy partners for their participation. Imagine their life force moving back into themselves as well, but you can allow the environment you share to reverberate to the Light and presence you have manifested for as long as it is able.

- Take a moment to once again stand in your Sovereignty, acknowledging your wholeness your integrity, your identity, and your connection to the Sacred. Then go about your daily affairs.

Julia's Commentary

Grail Space is created by invitation, hospitality and collaboration, all of which allow something to emerge that would not have been present otherwise. The Grail Space process acknowledges the life force within all things and seeks to partner with it.

When I am 'holding' something, as we discussed in the previous chapter, I am creating a space in which I can give love and blessing to something or someone I care about. When I shift my attention to a larger field of caring, I might feel it is too big for me to hold. Engagement with Grail Space is inviting the life within the room to join with me in creating a holding space. I am held as I hold. Thus the blessing field created emerges from a partnership which gives it the capacity to hold with more stability and grace.

When I focus, I can feel myself holding in the core of my body, from my throat to my sacrum. It is a warmth which fills my body and extends into my legs and feet, arms and hands. I often find myself touching things as I pass them, saying hello to the life within them. But Grail Space is much larger. It is the space in the room I am moving through, filled with so many expressions of sacred life. All this joins with me in holding space. When I was trying to write about holding, I realized that I have become so accustomed to inviting Grail Space that I cannot hold without doing it within Grail Space. It was hard to separate the one from the other.

So, here is the difference. Holding is creating a place for emergence; it is not necessarily sacred. Grail Space is intentionally supporting the emergence of the sacred. It is a conscious act of inviting the participation of the life around us to create a holding space for sacredness, which is why it is named for the legendary sacred vessel, the Holy Grail.

Grail Space feels like I am not only holding, but I am being held by the sacredness of the room and the house I am in. Or if I am walking through the forest, I notice the trees, moss, ferns, birds and critters - all the life around me - in its sacredness, and I invite them all to partner with me in blessing. A chalice is a wonderful image for it. And together we hold space for the beingness of the forest, and for the blessing field it offers to all those who move through it. I recognize the boundary of the forest, appreciate what it is, separate from myself, I feel the holding space it creates and extend my love and blessing to join with it.

What is the purpose of Grail Space? There is a gifting that humanity can offer to the earth, and as a consciously incarnate person, you can actively participate in that gifting. 'Seeing' the sacredness of all the earth and all the things upon it helps these things to be heightened in their own experience of sacredness and allows us to co-create a space of sacred blessing. As I get more accustomed to standing in Grail Space, it becomes second nature, and allows me to be more present to where I am. It is like being mindful but with the added sense of participation.

Grail Space is a way of creating a cup of holding for the sacred body of the earth and of yourself, a way of grounding your incarnational intent into a sacred holding of blessing. It enlists the aid of those things around you to increase the capacity of your holding, and to stabilize and ground your blessing field.

CHAPTER TEN:
THE INCARNATIONAL FIRE

In the preceding chapters and the exercises, I've presented three central concepts: Sovereignty, Self-Light, and Love. The interaction of these three in our lives produces and holds our "incarnational fire"; through them we express our generative self, our capacity to be a sun—a radiant star—in our lives and not simply a planet reflecting light from elsewhere.

In discussing the ideas of the Incarnational System and the mediated identity, my intent has been to show that incarnation is much more than just a soul slipping into and running around in a body, like a driver getting into a car and driving it about. Instead, the incarnational process is one of gathering and holding a diverse number elements and creating the conditions that enable them to converge and work together with integration and coherency. I call this gathering and synthesis holopoiesis, which means simply "the impulse or process of producing wholeness." But the active force behind holopoiesis making it possible is love, the love of the soul for its personal self, the love of the soul for the world it is engaging.

My point, therefore, has been to show just how deeply we are the products of love-in-action, bounded by Sovereignty and radiating Self-Light.

THE GENERATIVE SELF

SOVEREIGNTY

In other words, when we seek to bring love into our world, it is already there in the fabric of our incarnational nature. Ultimately, it is the force that makes incarnation possible. It is the spark that gives birth to our incarnational fire.

However, there is more to incarnation than the underlying actions of love emanating from the soul. When we take embodiment on the earth, something magical and alchemical begins to happen. A new self, a new identity, a new presence that is neither entirely soul nor entirely earth begins to emerge. This emergent incarnational identity is who we are.

At the simplest, most obvious level, this identity is our personality, our everyday self. But it contains within itself the power of its generative presence. The Presence Exercise is intended to be a portal into this presence. The magic of this presence is that, born of a deep incarnational alchemy, it is itself an alchemical, magical power that can stimulate transformation and emergence in the world around it.

One tool for doing this is Grail Space, the collaborative interaction with the life force embodied in all the things and beings that make up any given environment in which we are present and participating. By using the technique of Holding, we can create an alchemical Grail Space in which our soul meets the life and soul of the world—soul "stuff" joining with world "stuff"—in an act of loving partnership that allows something new to emerge. In this "incarnational alchemy", we bring into being both a new experience of the self and a new experience of the world. We become co-creators, co-incarnators with the life around us. In a way, we become incubators for the emergent expression of Gaia, the World Soul.

Seeing the world as a partner in bringing forth new capabilities of spirit and life, a blend of the gifts of the soul with the gifts of the Earth, contrasts sharply with the notion that the world and all the things on it are simply a backdrop, a stage setting, for us to work out our own human dramas. In the latter view, we isolate ourselves from the world or view it simply as a collection of resources at our peril, as the challenges of climate change, the rising of the oceans, the ongoing extinction of plant and animal species, and other developing environmental problems indicate.

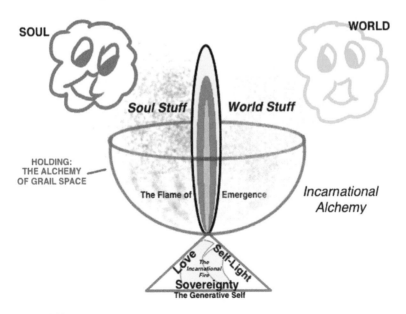

For me, the gift of incarnation is that we can be a presence in the world that brings new energies of spirit and life into being. We are a generative presence within the world, and together we light and hold a flame of emergence.

There are many voices in the world that try to tell us who we are and of what we are capable. All too often these voices undersell us, giving us images of ourselves and of the world that are limited, obstructive, and crippling. There is little joy in such images. We are variously identified as consumers, as sinners, as meaningless random accumulations of atoms, as followers of this or that individual or cause. Rarely are we seen as generative, radiant stars in our own right, not simply as a philosophical idea or an empowering image but because the very process of incarnation is one of generativity and presence.

For me, Incarnational Spirituality is an alternative to those voices and those images that would diminish both our lives and the life of the world that embraces and holds us. It is an alternative that moves away from philosophies that pit one part of us against another or that pit us against the world. It is an alternative that celebrates our ability to create wholeness in ourselves and in the environments around us.

The essence of Incarnational Spirituality is that we are generative sources of life, Light, and sacredness. We incarnate into a whole world that is both physical and non-physical. We can relate lovingly, creatively, and collaboratively with both these aspects of the world out of the power and fire of our generative nature. We are caretakers of this world and help foster its emerging life and potentials. We are incubators of Gaia.

Each of us is a unique manifestation of a generative self. There is no one else who engages the earth in the same way and makes possible the kind of emergence that results from the engagement with our sovereign individuality. We are each priceless partners with the life of the world. We are each practitioners of a unique incarnational alchemy.

Incarnation provides its challenges without doubt. We become part of a world with many problems, a world beset by a lack of love in too many places. Incarnation can seem a burden, a doorway to suffering and loss. There is no denying that incarnation is an "extreme sport", filled with risk. But it is also filled with reward. Nowhere else can the soul strengthen its muscles of creating wholeness and integration in quite the same way. Mastering the Incarnational System and the mediated identity is no small task, yet each of us do it all the time, everyday.

It's time we honored ourselves for being incarnate and learned to appreciate the privilege and the power of being embodied in a rich, diverse, hospitable world like this one. It's time we honored our capacity to be partners with the world, not its masters nor its servants. It's time to understand that incarnation is an exercise in collaboration.

When we engage our world with appreciation, with love, and with honor in recognition of what it brings to us—and when we likewise appreciate ourselves with the same love and honor in recognition of our generative presence—then we will truly be practicing a spirituality of incarnation. In reality, it's a spirituality of the co-incarnation of ourselves and the world together. When we realize this, we will have journeyed to the heart and Light of our Incarnational Fire.

Julia's Commentary

At the simplest, most obvious level, this (emergent incarnational) identity is our personality, our everyday self. But it contains within itself the power of its generative presence. The Presence Exercise is intended to be a portal into this presence. The magic of this presence is that, born of a deep incarnational alchemy, it is itself an alchemical, magical power that can stimulate transformation and emergence in the world around it.

We can live our lives, be successful and happy, and be a grace upon the planet without being consciously aware of or intentionally focusing upon the generative presence. We all know individuals who are radiant, loving, giving people who know nothing about an incarnational system, or a flame of emergence. They are a gift in and of themselves and are a blessing to those around them. But when we can make ourselves whole, gathering our parts into a coherence which is conscious and intentional, we open the portal to the presence of the soul. In this presence, we can experience the love that initiated our incarnation. This wholeness creates the stability in our personal self which allows the generative presence David talks about to be mediated into the world. Our capacity to love and to stimulate transformation is expanded.

What we are seeking here is a conscious and purposeful development of the capacity to hold in our lives this fire at the center of our incarnate selves. This is the capacity to be able to partner with our world from a place of powerful recognition of that deep love that is the source of our selves. This makes us more able to participate in blessing, healing and enlivening the larger field that is the world. Because we are each a unique outworking of this incarnational process, the contribution we make to the whole is irreplaceable, and when we can do this as a living practice, we can be more effective in partnering with the earth.

Each of us is a unique manifestation of a generative self. There is no one else who engages the earth in the same way and makes possible the kind of emergence that results from the engagement with our sovereign individuality. We are each priceless partners with the life of the world. We are each practitioners of a unique incarnational alchemy (which carries at its heart "the Light of our incarnational Fire").

ABOUT THE PUBLISHER

Lorian Press is a private, for profit business which publishes works approved by the Lorian Association. Current titles can be found on the Lorian website www.lorian.org.

The Lorian Association is a not-for-profit educational organization. Its work is to help people bring the joy, healing, and blessing of their personal spirituality into their everyday lives. This spirituality unfolds out of their unique lives and relationships to Spirit, by whatever name or in whatever form that Spirit is recognized.

For more information, go to www.lorian.org.

Lightning Source UK Ltd.
Milton Keynes UK
UKHW050920190822
407499UK00006B/238

9 780936 878768